# Marcia DeCoster's
# BEADS IN MOTION

## 24 JEWELRY PROJECTS THAT
## SPIN, SWAY, SWING, AND SLIDE

LARK JEWELRY
& BEADING

## LARK JEWELRY & BEADING

An Imprint of Sterling Publishing
387 Park Avenue South
New York, NY 10016

ISBN 978-1-4547-0335-8

Distributed in Canada by Sterling Publishing
c/o Canadian Manda Group, 165 Dufferin Street
Toronto, Ontario, Canada M6K 3H6
Distributed in the United Kingdom by GMC Distribution Services
Castle Place, 166 High Street, Lewes, East Sussex, England BN7 1XU
Distributed in Australia by Capricorn Link (Australia) Pty. Ltd.
P.O. Box 704, Windsor, NSW 2756, Australia

For information about custom editions, special sales, and premium and corporate purchases, please contact Sterling Special Sales at 800-805-5489 or specialsales@sterlingpublishing.com.

Email academic@larkbooks.com for information about desk and examination copies.
The complete policy can be found at larkcrafts.com.

Manufactured in China

2 4 6 8 10 9 7 5 3 1

larkcrafts.com

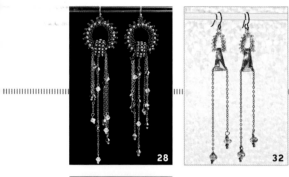

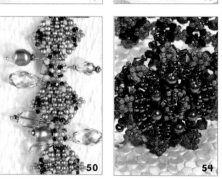

# CONTENTS

87

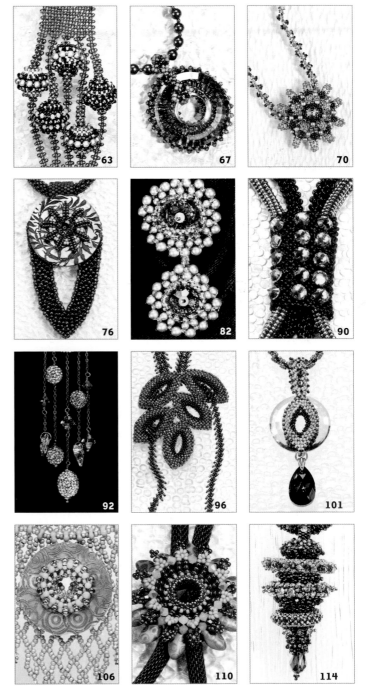

63 67 70

76 82 90

92 96 101

106 110 114

# INTRODUCTION

Motion was an early theme in my beadwork. Over time, I decided to explore creating a collection in which every piece of jewelry would include an element of movement. It became an interesting challenge that informed many of my decisions as a design came to life. This book brings together an array of projects that have both motion and beauty.

Some of the projects spin or slide, while for others the motion is as simple as the movement of fringe suspended from chain. In Swing Dance, for example, you can pull the crystal-studded chains to differing lengths. In Victorian Slide, pearl-encrusted medallions slide along a length of cubic right angle weave.

Rings of Saturn was one of my first serious efforts focusing on motion. Originally designed in 1997, it has long been a favorite of my students. I love people's reaction as they discover that each of the rings moves freely around the shaped ridges of the beaded center. The movement brings a sense of delight and playfulness to the piece.

Wanting to capture more of that joy, I designed Carousel, which features a unique ladder-stitched circle of beads that spins around a central post. The "spinner" invites play, so I made the piece into a bracelet to allow the wearer to interact with that element of the beadwork.

As the idea for each piece evolved, I explored which stitch would best serve the design's structure. In these projects, you'll find a broad range of stitches, including peyote, netting, cubic right angle weave, chevron, and many more. The Fundamentals chapter serves as a reference, if needed, to give you a basic understanding of each of the stitches.

One of the concepts I use in my design process is the idea of re-usable components. After designing a small bit of beadwork, I often find myself tempted to bead it again in other shades or with different materials, maybe changing out crystals for pearls or beading it in size 8° seed beads rather than size 11°s. This allows me to continue exploring color and texture using an already-perfected thread path.

The resulting designs may end up quite dissimilar. For example, Carousel and Riveted both use circular ladder stitch to create the spinner, but they look significantly different. In some cases, like the Gabriella series, the designs repeat an element and relate to one another, becoming a collection. The colors I have selected emphasize this association.

In fact, I chose a few limited palettes to bead the jewelry in this book, so the pieces complement one another when worn together. However, my hope is you'll bead them in your favorite colors, some bright, some muted, some neutral, and some dramatic.

You might choose to make a project exactly as it appears on these pages. Or you may fall in love with a particular component and bring your own creative vision to the design by using that component in different ways or with different materials. Either way, have fun exploring the key concepts of *Marcia DeCoster's Beads in Motion*—movement, re-usable design components, and your favorite colors!

# Chapter 1
# TOOLS & SUPPLIES

The art of beadweaving requires a simple tool kit. Needle, thread, scissors, a working surface, and beads—these are the most basic requirements, and all that's truly needed to create beautiful work. Within each of these categories, there's an array of choices, which may be explored for the varying results that each will bring. I've come to believe that most decisions that affect our beadwork come down to personal choice and perhaps the development of habits. During the course of my own beading career, I've changed my way of working from single to double thread, from not waxing to waxing, and from using Silamide to using FireLine, although these aren't hard and fast rules. They're merely the personal preferences that I've become comfortable with, so I encourage you to become familiar with the various styles and preferences of others who guide your explorations and to develop a set of protocols that work for you.

# Tools

I have a small list of tools that I consider essential and carry with me whenever I bead outside of the studio.

## Needles

Needles come in a range of sizes, designated with numbers. Most common are sizes 10, 11, 12, and 13, with the larger numbers being the thinner needles. The standard needle is 2 inches (5.1 cm) long. A shorter needle, referred to as a "sharp," measures 1¼ inches (3.2 cm). I generally use a 2-inch-long (5.1 cm) size 11 needle for most of my beadweaving. Occasionally, small beads with multiple thread passes through them will dictate the use of a size 13. If I'm weaving a piece where the beads are in tight formation, as in a layered right angle weave, I'll use a sharp for its ability to get into tight spaces. Newer needles have been developed which have a better resistance to bending and a longer span of use. If bent needles are an issue for you, these may be a consideration.

## Scissors

When cutting nylon thread, I favor my small, special-edition Gingher scissors for the fanciful patterns on their handle and their slim, sharp blades. When the job is to cut braided fishing line, a pair of children's Fiskars stands up best without dulling. Another option for cutting thread ends close to the work is a thread burner—a device that melts the thread with pinpoint precision. It's best to use traditional scissors to cut as close as possible, and *then* apply the tip of the burner to the remaining thread.

## Work Surfaces

There are a number of beautifully designed bead mats on the market today; these help contain beads and make them available to our needle and thread. For years, I've used a shallow leather jewelry tray with a velvet pad insert.

This allows projects in progress to be moved from room to room or stored between sessions. I have both light- and dark-colored velvet pads for use with different palettes. For travel I tend to use a more portable roll-up bead mat made of brightly colored fabrics and lined with Vellux, which provides a nonslip beading surface.

## Awl

Although it's perhaps not essential, a very fine-tipped awl is invaluable for untangling thread knots, pulling back beadwork in the event of a mistake, and breaking any incorrectly placed beads. If you've woven past the point of being able to take out the beadwork and discover an extra bead, it's easily broken without compromising the thread by inserting the tip of the awl into the hole and pushing the bead down onto the wider part of the awl.

## Triangular Bead Scoop

I carry a number of these in my tool kit, both for counting and for picking up unused beads to return them to their container.

## Needle Pull

A small piece of surgical tubing makes a handy needle pull for coaxing your needle through a small-hole bead. A small pair of pliers will do the trick handily as well.

## Thread Catcher

I like keeping my immediate surroundings free of culled beads or bits of thread while I work, so I always keep a thread catcher in a cheerful fabric nearby. Mine has a pincushion that rests close by on the edge of my worktable, keeping several needles nearby. A band of ribbon holds my scissors, and the fabric basket catches all of my untidy bits and pieces.

# Supplies

The majority of supplies used in the projects for *Marcia DeCoster's Beads in Motion* are readily available at your local bead store or favorite online bead source. In most cases, you can find a substitution that works well with the design. If you're unable to locate a supply and prefer not to make a substitution, check my website for a list of sources at www.marciadecoster.com/beadsinmotion/sourcelist.

## Thread

I consider thread choice to be a personal preference. The type of bead and type of stitch you use will help dictate the best choice for your work. If I'm working peyote stitch with cylinder beads, I'm apt to select one of the many brands of nylon thread available. Size D is standard and serves most of my needs. I may decide on a nylon thread if I want to use the thread color as part of the design element or if I want it to be a neutral backdrop to the woven beads.

When I'm using beads that may be prone to cutting the thread, like crystals or metal beads, I use a braided fishing line in a 6-pound test. There's a limited palette of colors in fishing line, but I find that smoke and crystal are both neutral enough to complement most bead color choices.

## Wax

I've taken to waxing my beading thread lately. I find I like that my two strands of thread are held closely together, resulting in fewer tangles. I use beeswax to wax FireLine and a microcrystalline wax for nylon thread. For some projects, the wax also provides that extra grab that helps the beads stay in position as the design develops. This seems especially true with larger beads and with stitches where the beads' ends aren't immediately adjacent to one another, as in right angle weave.

## Beads

There's a huge breadth of choice when it comes to the beads used for weaving. The majority of my work takes advantage of the uniformity and quality of Japanese seed beads and Swarovski crystals. I also like the diversity of adding some of the intriguing shapes and finishes available from Czech bead makers. Color and finishes are a huge part of creating visual interest in your finished pieces.

### Seed Beads

My work primarily uses Japanese seed beads made of glass. The beads are sized from size 15° through size 3° (the little

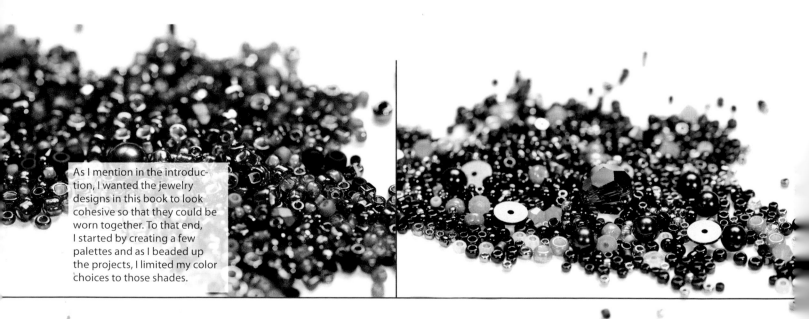

As I mention in the introduction, I wanted the jewelry designs in this book to look cohesive so that they could be worn together. To that end, I started by creating a few palettes and as I beaded up the projects, I limited my color choices to those shades.

degree symbol is pronounced "ott"), with the larger numbers signifying smaller beads. There's a wide variety of colors and finishes available, including matte, matte metallic, translucent, opaque, color-lined, and aurora borealis (AB) coatings. In recent years, much work has been done to increase the stability of surface colors, resulting in some beautiful color choices.

Most of the beads I use are round, with the occasional use of the cylindrical bead, which is more barrel-like in shape. These fit together nicely when using peyote stitch, and they make wonderful embellishment beads between the stitches of right angle weave.

There's also a category of seed beads made entirely of metal. These are uniformly sized brass beads plated with various metallic finishes, including copper, zinc, brass, and silver.

### Crystal Beads

There are a number of brands of crystals on the market. I personally use a variety of Swarovski Elements, including the crystal Xilion bead, whose many facets capture the light so beautifully. The Swarovski company, located in Austria, produces high-quality, precision-cut crystals in many beautiful

shapes and styles. Also featured in many of my designs are glass beads with a finish that imitates pearls. Swarovski's crystal pearls, which come in many colors and sizes, are excellent for beadweaving because of their uniform size.

### Czech Glass Beads

During manufacture, many Czech glass beads are pressed into molds and then tumbled to remove the edges that result from the molding process. Some of my favorites are the daggers, which are an excellent shape for many design considerations. The peacock finish imprints a design on the surface of the dagger and adds to its appeal. Beads referred to as fire-polished have a faceted surface and come in a large selection of colors and finishes.

### Findings

These include ear wires, eye pins and head pins, closure mechanisms, and so on. Feel free to use any clasps, bails, and spacers that work well with the design. I use a line of cast-pewter findings from Tierra Cast that are electroplated with gold, silver, and rhodium. Clasps, bails, spacers, and charms are part of the collection.

# Chapter 2
# FUNDAMENTALS

I've used a variety of stitches to weave the designs that I'm presenting to you in this book. Some of the projects focus on a single stitch, and some incorporate two or more different ones. The stitches used will be indicated in the project directions. In this chapter, I provide you with basic information on how to weave them. For simplicity, I've used size 11° beads in the illustrations, with the occasional size 8° seed bead or crystal when needed to illustrate a point. I feel in any craft it's important to have a good set of fundamental skills and what I present here is intended to assist you in learning the stitches you'll use—or to provide you with a refresher.

Three stitches, which I consider modified versions of ladder stitch and right angle weave, you may not have seen previously. They are documented on page 22 as Circular under the Ladder Stitch heading; as Diamonds under Right Angle Weave on page 18; and as Embellishment Beads under Right Angle Weave on page 17. Although adding an embellishment bead between the units of right angle weave isn't new, you may not be familiar with the method of adding the bead as part of the original weave.

As in my discussion on tools and supplies, I think there's a wide range of possible choices when considering the way in which we weave beads together. I've listened to many very accomplished artists describe their working process, and although it differs greatly from my own, it results in beautifully finished pieces of beadwork. So I encourage you to try various methods of working and arrive at a set of practices that serves you well. I list here the way in which I work as one point of reference.

# Beginning and Ending

- Most often I work with two wingspans of thread, which I thread onto a size 11 needle and then double. (When I'm using small beads and making multiple thread passes, I use a size 13 needle.) I wax both halves of thread, running them through beeswax from the needle toward the ends.

- Based on the project's requirements, I may opt to use single thread. When that's the case, I've indicated it in the project directions. It may be that I want a piece with softer drape or I know the thread will make several passes through a bead, so I choose not to fill up the thread holes with double thread.

- Generally, I forgo a stop bead, choosing instead to wrap the tail end of the thread around my little finger to prevent beads from falling off the thread. In the case of an especially large number of strung beads, however, I opt for a stop bead, which is done by picking up a bead and passing through it again to secure it and prevent subsequent beads from sliding off. The instructions will tell you when to add one.

- In right angle weave, I tie a knot to secure the first four beads into a circle and weave through beads to exit one away from the knot before starting my weave.

- When beginning and ending threads, I weave through beads in the pattern of the stitch I am weaving, tying a half-hitch knot once or twice between beads, then passing through a few beads away from the knot before trimming the ends.

# Knots

You'll use these knots with some frequency when beadweaving.

## Overhand Knot

Create a loop with the thread. Pass the tail through the loop and pull to tighten (figure 1).

**figure 1**

## Square Knot

Using both ends of the thread, pass one thread under, over, and under the other thread. Pull to tighten.

Repeat passing the same thread under, over and under the other thread and pull to tighten (figure 2).

**figure 2**

## Half-Hitch

Pass under the thread between two beads. Pull gently to create a loop. Pass back over the thread and pass through the loop from the underside. Pull to tighten (figure 3).

**figure 3**

## Peyote Stitch

### Flat, Even

**1** Pick up an even number of beads (which will become rows 1 and 2) to equal the length of the piece.

**2** Pick up one bead and pass back through the second-to-last bead added. Continue to pick up one bead, skip one bead, and pass through the next bead. This forms row 3 (figure 4).

**figure 4**

**3** The beads will now be oriented with one high bead and one low bead across the row. Pick up one bead and pass through the first high bead in the previous row. Continue picking up one bead and passing through the next high bead across the row (figure 5).

**figure 5**

### Joining or "Zipping Up"

To create a tube of peyote stitch with even edges, bead a flat piece and then join the two edges of the high and low beads. (You'll need an even number of rows so that the high and low beads fit into one another.) Exiting from a bead on one side of the join, pass through the corresponding bead on the opposite edge. Continue to alternate, passing through one bead on the top edge and one bead on the bottom edge, until all are joined (figure 6).

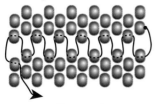

**figure 6**

## Tubular, Even

**1** To maintain a soft tension when creating a ring of peyote stitch, begin with the desired number of beads and work flat peyote stitch for three rounds.

**2** Join the two ends of the beadwork into a ring by weaving from the single bead through one side of the two beads on the opposite end. Turn and pass through the second of the two beads, back through the original bead, and then the next bead. This is called a step up (figure 7).

**figure 7**

**3** Pick up one bead and pass through the next high bead. Continue around, stepping up through the first bead added in this round (figure 8).

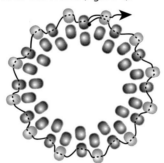

**figure 8**

When working a smaller tube, instead of following the procedure described in step 1, pick up the desired number of beads and tie an overhand knot to create a circle. Pick up one bead, skip a bead, and pass through the next bead. Step up at the end of the round. Continue working rounds for the desired length.

## Right Angle Weave

### Flat

**1** Follow along with figure 9. Pick up four beads and tie an overhand knot to form a circle. Pass through one bead to clear the knot. This is the first unit.

**2** Pick up three beads and pass through the last bead exited and the first two beads just added; repeat for the desired length.

**3** Weave through the beads to exit from a top bead at the end of the row. Pick up three beads; pass through the last top bead exited and continue weaving through beads to exit from the side bead just added that sits toward the work.

• For the first unit of every row, you will add three beads. The second and all subsequent units require adding only two beads because the units share both the side bead from the previous unit and the bottom bead from the previous row.

• In right angle weave you alternate between working clockwise and counterclockwise. Depending on how you start—up or down from the first side bead—and how many units you complete, the direction you're going may be different from the one shown in the illustration.

• If your thread is exiting up from a side bead, then you'll pick up two beads and travel counterclockwise through the next bottom bead, the side bead of the previous unit, and the top and side beads of the new unit. If your thread is exiting down from a side bead, then pass through the next bottom bead, pick up two beads, and travel clockwise through the previous side bead, the bottom bead, and the new side bead. Alternate between these two steps until the row is completed.

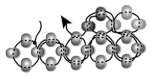

**figure 9**

## Joining

To form a flat piece of right angle weave into a tube, align two opposite edges. Exiting up through a side bead, pick up a top bead, pass through the opposite side bead, pick up a bottom bead, and then pass through the first side bead, the new top bead, the opposite side bead, the new bottom bead, and the next side bead. Subsequent units require only one bead to complete the unit (figure 10). **Note:** As mentioned previously, your thread may not exit the side bead from the top, as indicated in this illustration. In that case, you would add the bottom bead first and then the top bead.

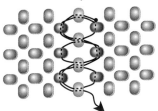

**figure 10**

## Tubular

**1** Work the desired number of units of flat right angle weave, minus one.

**2** Exiting from the side bead of the last unit, pick up one bead and pass through the side bead of the first unit. Pick up one bead and pass through the side bead of the last unit, the bottom bead just added, the side bead of the first unit, and the top bead just added to form a ring. To begin the next round, pick up three beads and pass through the last bead exited, the three beads just added, and the next top bead of the previous round (figure 11).

**figure 11**

**3** Complete the round, adding two beads for each unit until you have only one bottom bead left. This is the last unit. It will share the side bead from the first unit, the side bead from the previous unit, and the bottom bead from the previous row. Only one bead will be required to complete this unit (figure 12).

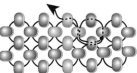

**figure 12**

## Embellishment Beads

Typically, embellishment beads are added after the right-angle-weave fabric is created. You pass through a bead on the base, pick up a bead, and pass through the next bead on the base. This results in added structure to the piece. However, there are times when I prefer to add that bead while I'm weaving the original base. I find this maintains the fluidity of the fabric and each unit can be woven in the same direction, passing less thread through the holes, which also contributes to fluidity.

**1** Follow along with figure 13. Create the first row of right angle weave to the desired length.

**2** For row 2, unit 1, pick up three beads and pass through the last bead exited. Pick up one bead and pass through the next top bead of the previous row. Pick up two beads and travel clockwise through the side bead of the previous unit and the following top bead of the previous row.

**3** Continue to the end of the row, always traveling clockwise and picking up one bead before entering the next top bead.

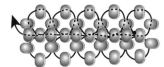

**figure 13**

## Circular

Circular right angle weave differs from tubular right angle weave in that the size or the number of beads in a unit are used to create a flat circle of beadwork as opposed to a tube.

Begin by stitching a flat piece of right angle weave that is the desired number of units minus one. Join the two ends by adding a top and bottom bead as in tubular right angle weave (figure 14).

**figure 14**

Add extra units as in tubular right angle weave, but increase either the size or the number of beads at the top of the unit to maintain a flat surface (figure 15).

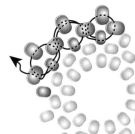

**figure 15**

## Layered

**1** Weave a base of right angle weave to the desired size. You can leave the work flat or join it into a tube.

**2** Exiting from a bead on the base, pick up one bead and pass through the next bead on the base. Repeat for the desired number of rows (figure 16).

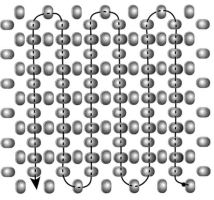

**figure 16**

**3** Exit from one of the beads added in step 2. Pick up one bead and pass through the opposite bead. Pick up one bead and pass through the original bead, the first bead added, and the opposite bead. Repeat across the row and for additional rows as desired (figure 17).

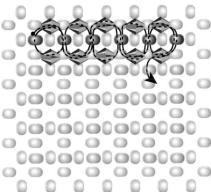

**figure 17**

## Diamonds

This stitch is like right angle weave in that it has a shared bead and alternates between working clockwise and working counterclockwise. The interior beads added to the circle cause the exterior beads to form a diamond shape.

**1** Pick up the following sequence four times: three outside beads and one accent bead. Tie a square knot to join the beads into a circle (figure 18).

**figure 18**

**2** Pass through the first accent bead. Pick up one interior bead and pass through the next accent bead. Repeat three times (figure 19), pulling tightly after each bead. The outside beads will form a diamond shape (figure 20).

**figure 19**

**figure 20**

**3** To add more diamonds, weave through the beads to the middle of one group of three outside beads. Pick up one outside bead, one accent bead, three outside beads, and one accent bead. Repeat the group of three outside beads and one accent bead twice more and pick up one outside bead. Pass through the last bead exited on the previous unit, the next outside bead, and the first accent bead (figure 21). Add interior beads as described in step 2.

**figure 21**

# Cubic Right Angle Weave

Traditional right angle weave is worked with four beads in each unit. The number of beads to a side may vary, but they're treated as one. I think of them as bottom, side, top, and side. In cubic right angle weave, there are six surfaces in each cube, with each surface consisting of the four beads as described above. I think of the surfaces as a floor, four walls, and a ceiling. For the sake of simplicity, we'll work here with one bead to a side of each unit.

**1** To build the floor, pick up four beads and tie an overhand knot. Pass through one bead to clear the knot (figure 22).

**figure 22**

**2** To build the first wall, pick up three beads and pass through the last floor bead exited. Here's where we depart from traditional right angle weave. Instead of passing through the side bead, you'll pass through the next floor bead. Right now the three new beads are on the same plane as the floor; however, like a tip-up building, in a few stitches this section will be pulled into an upright position at a right angle to the floor (figure 23).

**figure 23**

**3** As in traditional right angle weave, you have a bottom bead in place from the floor and you now have a side bead in place from the first wall. To build the second wall, pick up a side and a top bead and pass through the side bead from the first wall, the bottom bead, and the next bottom bead (figure 24).

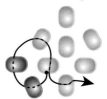

**figure 24**

**4** The third wall is built the same as the second wall, with the addition of a side and a top bead. This is again where we depart from the traditional weave, in that we're always moving in the same direction rather than alternating between clockwise and counterclockwise. After passing through the next bottom bead, you will also pass through the side bead from the first wall (figure 25).

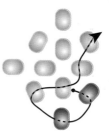

**figure 25**

**5** You now have a side bead from the first wall, a bottom bead, and a side bead from the third wall. To build the fourth wall, pick up one top bead and pass through the side bead of the third wall, the bottom bead, the side bead of the first wall, and the top bead of the first wall (figure 26). At this point a gentle pull on the thread will bring up the four walls, and the tops of these walls will create the ceiling of the first cube and the floor of the next cube. *Note*: You will see some cubic right angle weave directions that take one additional pass through the top four beads after the walls are in place. I don't take this extra step because beading the next set of walls essentially puts this same thread in place. If it helps you to see the top of the cube better, then by all means try this approach.

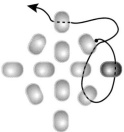

**figure 26**

**6** Exiting from the top bead (now a floor bead for the next cube), build the next cube by repeating steps 2 to 5. Figure 27 shows the first three beads for the first wall, the same as in figure 23, and also shows the side beads that are in place from the first cube.

**figure 27**

If you're making a length of cubic right angle weave one cube wide, then continue to repeat steps 2 to 5 for the desired length.

## Building Width

Once you've achieved the number of cubes you desire in length, it's possible to begin creating cubes off of any of the four walls. In this example, I build three cubes in width.

**1** Turn the work so that three walls face you and the thread is exiting the bottom edge bead, which will become your new floor (figure 28).

**figure 28**

**2** Pick up three beads and pass through the last bead exited. This is your first wall (figure 29).

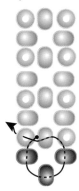

**figure 29**

**3** To complete the cube, repeat steps 2 to 5 of Cubic Right Angle Weave. When the fourth wall is built, pass through the next floor bead in the second cube (figure 30).

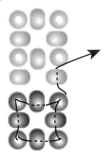

**figure 30**

**4** The second cube is a bit different. The first wall is shared with the first cube and is already in place. Only three walls need to be built. To build the second wall, pick up one side and one top bead, and then pass through the side bead from the fourth wall of the first cube, the floor bead, and the next floor bead (figure 31).

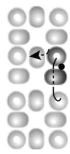

**figure 31**

**5** To build the third wall, pick up one side bead and one top bead. Pass through the side bead from the second wall, the bottom bead, the next bottom bead, and the side bead from the second wall of the first cube (figure 32).

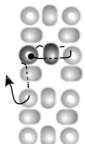

**figure 32**

**6** The fourth wall requires only one bead. Pick up one top bead and pass through the side bead of the third wall and the floor bead of the next cube (figure 33).

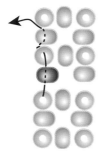

**figure 33**

**7** As in the second cube, the first wall of the third cube is already in place and only three walls need to be built. To build the second wall, pick up a side and a top bead and pass through the side bead of the fourth wall of cube 2, the floor bead, and the next floor bead (figure 34).

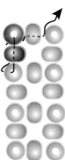

**figure 34**

**8** To build the third wall, pick up a side bead and a top bead. Pass through the side bead from the second wall, the floor bead, the next floor bead, and the side bead from the second wall of cube 2 (figure 35).

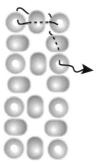

**figure 35**

**9** To build the fourth wall, pick up a top bead. Pass through a side bead from the third wall of the third unit, the floor bead of the third wall, the side bead, and the ceiling bead of the third wall (figure 36).

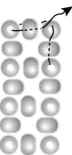

**figure 36**

You may build as many additional rows of cubes as you like, repeating steps 3 to 9.

# Ladder Stitch

## Flat and Tubular

Ladder stitch makes a convenient start for brick stitch and can also be used for herringbone stitch. When creating a small strip of ladder stitch, I often forgo the stop bead and wrap the tail around my little finger to keep the beads from escaping off the end of the thread.

**1** Pick up the desired number of beads. Pass through the second-to-last bead added (figure 37). Pull to align the two beads next to one another.

**figure 37**

**2** Pass through the next bead (figure 38) and pull to align; repeat for all beads.

**figure 38**

**3** To join the ladder-stitched strip into a ring, pass the working thread through the last bead of the strip, through the first bead, and through the last bead again (figure 39).

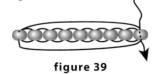

**figure 39**

You can make a two-bead-high ladder stitch by picking up the desired number of beads and passing through the third and fourth beads, counting from the working end, and then the next two beads for each subsequent stitch.

## Circular

In the previous example, all of the beads were pre-strung to create the ladder. In circular ladder stitch, the ladder stitch columns are pre-strung and additional beads are picked up to create tips and spacers between the columns. This stitch requires a fair amount of slack on your working thread. You may accomplish this by placing your working beads a few inches (5 or 6 cm) away from your stop bead, or by leaving a long tail and moving your stop bead as you require slack.

**1** Pick up a bead and pass back through it to form a stop bead.

**2** Pick up three beads to make up half of the first spine, and three beads for the tip. For each additional spine desired, pick up six spine beads and three tip beads. Pick up three spine beads to complete the first spine. Counting from the working end, and passing through beads from the tail end, pass through the three beads in the first spine and the first bead of the tip beads (figure 40).

**figure 40**

**3** Pull to align the beads into columns. Pick up five tip beads, skip the middle tip bead, and pass through the next tip bead and the three spine beads below it. Pass up through the adjacent column of the spine (figure 41).

**figure 41**

**4** Pick up one accent bead and pass through the three spine beads on the working thread below the existing spine (figure 42).

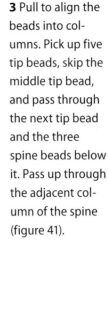
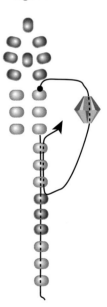

**figure 42**

**5** Pass through the first three of the six spine beads on the working thread and the next tip bead (figure 43).

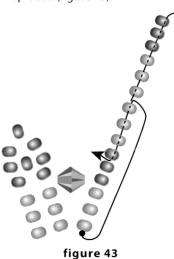

**figure 43**

**6** Repeat steps 3 to 5 until all working beads have been used. Pass through the first spine, pick up one accent bead, and pass through the last spine.

**7** To reinforce the shape and connect the top of the spines beneath the tips, weave up through one half of the spine beads and down through the other. Repeat around (figure 44).

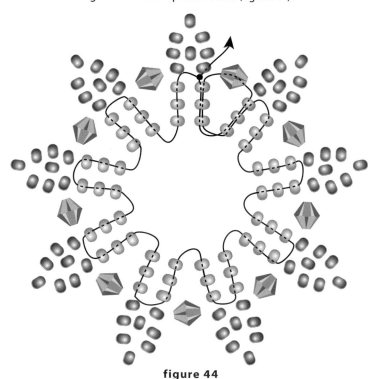

**figure 44**

## Chevron Stitch

**1** Follow along with figure 45. Pick up one bead and pass through it again. Pick up six beads and pass back through the first bead strung. *Note*: You may choose to pick up contrasting colors in a pattern, as shown in the illustration.

**2** Pick up four beads and pass through the fifth bead added in the first unit. Pick up four beads and pass back through the third bead added in the previous unit. Continue to pick up four beads and alternate between passing through the fifth bead and the third bead of the previous units.

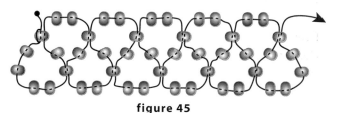

**figure 45**

# Herringbone Stitch

## Tubular

**1** Start by making a ladder-stitched strip with the desired number of units, remembering that each spine will have two columns.

**2** Connect the first and last beads of the strip to form a ring.

**3** Exiting from the top of a ladder-stitched bead, pick up two beads and pass down through the next bead of the ring and up through the following one; repeat around, stepping up through the first bead added (figure 46).

**figure 46**

It's possible to place beads of the same or smaller size between the spines as you weave them. Exiting from one of the columns on a spine, pick up two beads and pass down through the spine bead in the next column. Pick up one bead before passing up through the first column on the next group of spine beads. Repeat around and step up. You may add more beads for each round of herringbone stitch (figure 47).

**figure 47**

# Brick Stitch

## Flat

Start by making a ladder-stitched strip the desired width. Exiting from the edge bead of the strip, pick up two beads and pass under the thread between the first and second ladder-stitched beads and back through the second bead just added. Pick up one bead and pass under the thread between the second and third beads of the ladder-stitched strip (figure 48). Repeat to the end of the row. Turn and begin the next row adding two beads at the beginning of the row as shown in the illustration. Repeat across.

**figure 48**

## Decrease

Start by making a ladder-stitched strip the desired width. Exiting from the edge bead of the strip, pick up two beads and pass under the thread between the second and third ladder-stitched beads and back through the second bead just added. Pick up one bead and pass under the thread between the third and fourth beads of the ladder-stitched strip (figure 49). Repeat to the end of the row. Turn and begin the next row, adding two beads at the beginning of the row, as shown in the illustration. Repeat across.

**figure 49**

# Spiral Rope

There are many variations of this pretty stitch. This is one of the most basic ways to do it, but it can be easily varied by the type and count of the beads used on the outside beads.

**1** Pick up four core beads and three outside beads. Pass back through the four core beads and align the beads next to one another (figure 50).

**figure 50**

**2** Pick up one core bead and three outside beads. Pass through the three previous core beads and the one new core bead (figure 51).

**figure 51**

**3** Push the new group of three beads next to the previous group (figure 52). Continue to repeat steps 2 and 3 for the desired length.

**figure 52**

# Vertical Netting

Netting can be built off a base of another stitch. It's easiest to see the pattern if the shared bead is a contrasting color.

**1** Follow along with figure 53. Exiting from a base bead, pick up one contrasting bead, three of the main color, one of the contrasting color, and three of the main color. Repeat for the desired number of nets (in this case, three times). Pick up one contrasting color and three additional main beads to turn. Pass back through the last contrasting bead added to form a picot. Pick up three of the main color, one contrasting bead, and three of the main color. Pass back through the second contrasting bead of the last group. Pick up three of the main color, one contrasting bead, and three of the main color. Pass back through the second contrast bead from the one currently exited. Repeat for the number of nets. Pass through the next bead on the base.

**figure 53**

**2** Now refer to figure 54. Pick up one contrasting bead and three of the main color. Pass back through the next contrast bead from the previous vertical net. Pick up three of the main color, one contrasting color, and three of the main color. Pass back through the next contrasting bead on the previous vertical net. Pick up three of the main color, one contrasting color, and three additional main beads to turn. Pass back through the next contrasting bead just added to form a picot. Pick up three main color beads, one contrasting bead, and three main color beads. Pass back through the first unshared contrasting bead on the string of beads just added. Pick up three main color beads, one contrasting bead, and three main color beads. Pass back through the first contrasting bead and pass through the next base bead. Continue for the desired length.

**figure 54**

# St. Petersburg Chain

## Single

**1** Use double thread to pick up five beads. Pass through the first three beads (figure 55). Pull to align the beads into two columns.

**figure 55**

**2** Pick up one bead and one turning bead of a contrasting color. Pass back through the first bead just added and the three beads in the column below. Pick up one contrasting bead and pass up through the two beads in the next column (figure 56). (The last bead added in this stitch is your contrasting edge bead. It will be shared if you're making a double St. Petersburg chain, which is explained next.)

**figure 56**

**3** Pick up four beads and pass through the first two beads again (figure 57).

**figure 57**

**4** Pull to align the last four beads added into two columns. Pick up one bead and one contrasting bead. Pass back through the first bead just added and the three beads below it. Pick up one contrasting bead and pass up through the two beads in the next column (figure 58).

**figure 58**

Repeat steps 3 and 4 for the desired length.

## Double

**1** Work a single St. Petersburg chain to the desired length. This is side 1.

**2** Using a new double thread, start as in step 1 of single St. Petersburg chain, but this time let the three-bead column sit on the right-hand side. Pick up one bead and one contrasting bead. Pass back through the first bead just added and the three beads below. Pass through the inside edge bead from side 1 and the two beads in the next column (figure 59).

**figure 59**

**3** Pick up four beads and pass through the first and second beads again (figure 60).

**figure 60**

**4** Pull to align the last four beads added into two columns. Pick up one bead and one turning bead of a contrasting color. Pass back through the first bead just added and the three beads below. Pass through the next inside edge bead from side 1 and the two beads in the next column (figure 61).

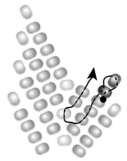

**figure 61**

Repeat steps 3 and 4 for the length of side one.

# Chapter 3
# EARRINGS & RINGS

Matte black size 15° seed beads, 2 g (A)

Gold-lined olivine rainbow size 15° seed beads, 1 g (B)

Metallic olive size 15° seed beads, 1 g (C)

Color-lined olivine size 11° seed beads, 1 g (D)

Green bronze size 11° seed beads, 2 g (E)

36 olivine cube beads, 2 mm (F)

10 jet crystal bicones, 4 mm

12 olivine crystal bicones, 4 mm

9 golden shadow crystal bicones, 4 mm

30 inches (76.2 cm) of fine black chain, 2 mm wide

14 black ball-end head pins, 2 inches (5.1 cm) long, 22 gauge

17 black eye pins, 22 gauge

2 black ear wires

Thread

Wax

Needles

Scissors

Wire cutters

Round-nose pliers

Chain-nose pliers

## FINISHED SIZE

4¼ inches (10.8 cm) long

## TECHNIQUES

Peyote stitch

Right angle weave

# SWING DANCE EARRINGS

Use peyote stitch to create and embellish a ring, then add a cascade of movable crystal-studded chain to form the liveliest earrings ever.

## Ring

**Rows 1 and 2:** Pick up 40 A beads (figure 1).

**figure 1**

**Row 3:** Pick up one A bead, skip one A bead of the previous row, and pass through the next A bead to form a peyote stitch; repeat for a total of 20 A beads to form a strip (figure 2).

**figure 2**

## THE WAY IT MOVES
Embellished with crystals, the dainty chains are a flashing, scintillating pendulum. They slide freely in the beaded bead holding them against the ring and can therefore be adjusted as desired.

Join the strip into a circle by passing through the top A bead on the opposite end and the A bead below it, then pass back through the last A bead exited on the other end and the next A bead to step up (figure 3). **Note:** This start ensures a softer result, as opposed to tying the original 40 beads into a circle. You'll now begin working in the round.

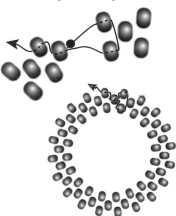

**figure 3**

**Rounds 4 and 5:** Work tubular peyote stitch using A beads for two rounds.

**Rounds 6–8:** Work tubular peyote stitch using E beads for three rounds (figure 4).

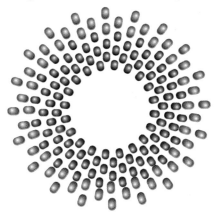

**figure 4**

**Round 9:** Weave through beads to exit from round 1. Work tubular peyote stitch using E beads (figure 5).

**figure 5**

**Round 10:** Work tubular peyote stitch using E beads.

**Zip:** Fold the beadwork so that the beads of round 10 and round 8 interlock. Weave the beads together to form a seamless join (figure 6).

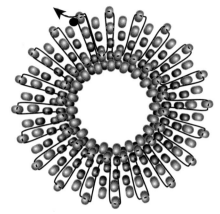

**figure 6**

**Embellish:** Exiting from an E bead of round 10, pick up one D bead, and pass through the next E bead; repeat to add a total of 20 D beads around the ring (figure 7).

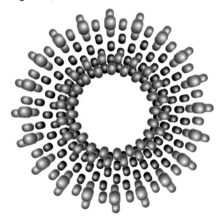

**figure 7**

Weave through beads to exit from an E bead of round 8 on the edge of the ring. Pick up one F bead and one C bead. Pass back through the F bead just added and through the next E bead of round 8 to form a fringe; repeat to add a total of 17 fringes (figure 8). **Note:** The empty space between the fringes leaves room for the beaded bead and chains added later.

**figure 8**

**Loop:** Weave through beads to exit from the E bead behind the top cube bead, opposite the empty space at the bottom of the ring. Pick up eight C beads and pass through the last E bead exited to form a loop (figure 9). Repeat the thread path to reinforce. Secure the thread and trim. Set the ring aside.

**figure 9**

## Beaded Bead

**Base:** Use single thread and C beads to work a strip of right angle weave three units wide and 11 rows long. Pass the strip through the ring around the unembellished section and then join the first row to the 11th row by adding side beads (figure 10).

**figure 10**

**Layer 1:** Exiting from an edge C bead, pick up one A bead and pass through the next C bead; repeat for the entire edge. Weave through beads to exit from the side C bead of the next row; repeat the embellishment with A beads. Repeat on the next rows for a total of four columns of A beads. **Note:** This layer will provide the side beads of the next round of right angle weave (figure 11).

**figure 11**

*Layer 2:* Work a round of tubular right angle weave using B beads for the bottom and top of each unit and the A beads from layer 1 as side beads for the two outside rows, and D beads for the bottom and top of each unit and the A beads from layer 1 as the side beads for the center row (figure 12). Don't trim the thread; exit from one D bead at the center of the beaded bead. Set aside.

**figure 12**

## Crystal Chains

*Chain 1:* Follow along with figure 13. Cut a ½-inch (1.3 cm) length of chain. Slide one olivine bicone onto a head pin. Use round-nose pliers and wire cutters to form a simple loop that connects to either end of the chain just cut. Slide one jet bicone onto an eye pin; form a simple loop that connects to the other end of the same chain. Cut a ¾-inch (1.9 cm) length of chain and connect it to the jet link just made. Slide a golden shadow bicone onto an eye pin; form a simple loop that connects to the other end of the chain just attached. Cut a piece of chain 1⅜ inches (3.5 cm) long and connect

one end to the golden shadow link just attached. Pass the open end of the chain through the beaded bead (figure 13).

**figure 13**

Slide one jet bicone onto an eye pin; form a simple loop that connects to the end of the chain just threaded through the beaded bead. Cut a ⅝-inch (1.6 cm) length of chain; attach the end link to the jet link just attached. Slide one olivine 4-mm bicone onto a head pin; form a simple loop that connects to the chain just attached. *Note:* The final chain should be about 5 inches (12.7 cm) long.

*Chains 2 and 3:* Repeat chain 1 twice, varying the bicone colors and the distances between links so that chain 2 uses two olivine and one jet bicone and is 3½ inches (8.9 cm) long, and so that chain 3 uses one olivine, one golden shadow, and one jet bicone and measures 4 inches (10.2 cm) long.

*Chain 4:* This is the chain that hangs from the beaded bead. Form a chain that uses two olivine, one golden shadow, and one

jet bicone and is 3 inches (7.6 cm) long; keep one end of this chain open—that side should not have a bead on a head pin. Use the working thread of the beaded bead to neatly and securely stitch the open end link of this chain to the D bead the thread is exiting (figure 14). Secure the thread and trim.

**figure 14**

## Ear Wire

Use chain-nose pliers to attach an ear wire to the loop at the top of the ring.

Repeat all steps to make a second earring. *Note:* Use the remaining bicones to make the crystal chains, and don't worry about matching them to the first earring.

# KEYSTONE EARRINGS

Beautiful keystone beads are the perfect centerpiece for a bit of embellished peyote stitch and lengths of free-swinging chain that fit perfectly through the bottom of these faceted trapezoidal crystal beads. End the chain with pretty briolette dangles that can be moved to symmetrical or asymmetrical lengths, as your design preference dictates.

## Top Loop

*Rows 1 and 2:* Use single thread to pick up 24 A beads.

*Row 3:* Pick up one A bead, skip one A bead of the previous round, and pass through the next A bead; repeat to the end of the row.

*Row 4:* Work 12 peyote stitches with one A bead in each stitch (figure 1).

**figure 1**

## THE WAY IT MOVES

Wear the chains at roughly even lengths, or pull them for an asymmetrical look. Either way, they'll swing, sway, and delight.

*Row 5:* Work 12 peyote stitches with one B bead in each stitch to form the curved shape (figure 2).

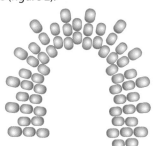

**figure 2**

*Crystal Embellishment, first side*: Weave through beads to exit from the second-to-last A of row 4, toward the work. Pick up one C bead and pass through the next A bead of row 4; repeat four times to exit from the center A bead of row 4.

*Ear-wire loop:* Pick up seven A beads and pass through the last A bead exited to form a loop.

*Crystal Embellishment, second side*: Pick up one C bead and pass through the next A bead of row 4; repeat four times (figure 3).

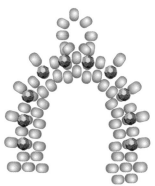

**figure 3**

## Keystone

Follow along with figure 4. Weave through beads to exit from an end A bead of row 1. Pick up three A beads and pass through the top of the keystone bead and through the A bead at the other end of row 1. Weave through beads to turn and repeat the thread path to reinforce. Secure the thread and trim.

## Finish

Cut a piece of chain 4½ inches (11.4 cm) long. Slide one bicone and one briolette bead onto a head pin. Form a wrapped loop with round-nose pliers, catching one end of the chain in it before you close it. Pass the other end of the chain through the bottom of the keystone bead. Slide one bicone and one briolette bead onto another head pin. Form a wrapped loop, catching the other end of the chain in it.

**figure 4**

Attach an ear wire to the seed bead loop completed at the top of the beadwork.

Repeat all steps to make a second earring.

## SUPPLIES

Light gray size 15° seed beads, 1 g (A)

Light gray size 11° seed beads, 1 g (B)

Dark silver size 11° seed beads, 1 g (C)

56 indigo crystal round beads, 2 mm (D)

28 light silver crystal pearl round beads, 3 mm (E)

28 light silver crystal pearl round beads, 4 mm (F)

2 indigo crystal-encrusted beads, 12 mm

2 silver shade crystal heart-shaped pendants, 12 x 10 mm

2 gunmetal ball-end head pins, 2 inches (5.1 cm) long, 22 gauge

2 pieces of fine gunmetal chain, each 1 inch (2.5 cm) long

2 gunmetal ear wires

Thread

Wax

Needles

Scissors

## FINISHED SIZE

1⅛ x 3⅜ inches (2.9 x 8.5 cm) long

## TECHNIQUES

Peyote stitch

Right angle weave

# GABRIELLA EARRINGS

Start these sparkling earrings with a woven circle of pearls and crystals. Add a bead encrusted with crystals to the center, then suspend a bit of thin chain tipped with a heart crystal that dances below your lobe.

## Medallion

*Round 1:* Thread 72 inches (1.8 m) of thread and double it. Pull one end of the thread so you have a 12-inch (30.5 cm) length of single thread. Pick up four A beads and position them 4 inches (10.2 cm) from the end of the doubled thread. Tie a double overhand knot. *Note:* The single tail thread will be used to complete rounds of peyote later in the process.

Complete 13 units of right angle weave and join the last unit to the first to form a ring with a total of 14 units. Exit from a top A bead.

*Round 2:* Work a round of tubular right angle weave using one A bead for each side and one B bead for the top of each unit. Exit from a top B bead.

*Round 3:* Work a round of tubular right angle weave using B beads. Exit from a top bead.

*Round 4:* Use one E bead and one C bead for each side and one F bead for the top of each unit.

## Embellish

*Round 5:* Weave through beads to exit from a B bead at the top of round 3. Pick up one D bead and pass through

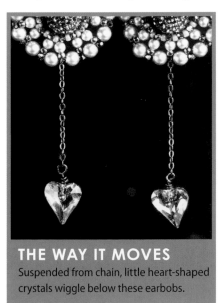

### THE WAY IT MOVES
Suspended from chain, little heart-shaped crystals wiggle below these earbobs.

the next B bead; repeat around. Weave through beads to exit from an F bead at the top of round 4.

*Round 6:* Pick up one D bead and pass through the next F bead; repeat around.

*Loop:* Weave through beads to exit from a C bead on the side of round 4. Pick up seven A beads and pass back through the last C bead exited, the pearl beneath it, and the nearest B bead at the top of round 3 to form a hanging loop to which you'll attach the ear wire later.

*Center:* Pick up one crystal-encrusted bead and pass through the B bead directly opposite the last B bead exited. Pass back through the crystal-encrusted bead and through the original B bead. Repeat the thread path to reinforce. Weave through beads to exit from a C bead directly opposite the hanging loop. Don't trim the working thread.

*Round 7 (back):* Weave the tail thread through beads to exit from a bottom A bead of round 1. Pick up one A bead and pass through the next two A beads of round 1. Step up through the first A bead added in this round.

*Round 8 (back):* Pick up one A bead and pass through the next A bead; repeat around for a total of seven beads. Step up through the first A bead added in this round.

*Round 9 (back):* Pick up one A bead and pass through the next two A beads; repeat once. Pick up one A bead and pass through the next three A beads. Pull the thread gently to tighten. Secure the tail thread and trim.

## Dangle

**1** Slide one heart pendant onto a head pin. Use chain-nose pliers to grasp the head pin at the back of the hole and form a 90° bend as close to the pendant as possible. Form a wrapped loop, catching the end link of one piece of

chain inside it before you close it. Use the remaining working thread from the medallion to pass through the other end link of the chain, and pass back through the last C bead exited (figure 1). Repeat the thread path to reinforce. Secure the thread and trim.

**figure 1**

**2** Attach an ear wire to the loop of seed beads at the top of the medallion.

Repeat all steps to make a second earring.

## BACK

## SUPPLIES

Blue iris size 15° seed beads, 1 g (A)

Dark silver size 15° seed beads, 1 g (B)

12 blue iris size 11° seed beads (C)

66 light metallic gold crystal rounds, 2 mm (D)

2 light gray crystal pearl rounds, 8 mm

2 black diamond crystal lochrose beads, 4 mm

2 silver ball-end head pins, 20 gauge

Thread

Wax

Needles

Scissors

Round-nose pliers

## FINISHED SIZE

1¾ inches (4.5 cm) long

## TECHNIQUES

Herringbone

Netting

# TRIPLE TWIRL EARRINGS

This pretty little design starts with an easy-to-make flared tubular herringbone-stitched base. Add spinning, twirling netting-stitched rings, string it all on a head pin with some beads, and you've got a great pair of earrings.

## Base

Using single thread, pick up 12 A beads, leaving a 6-inch (15.2 cm) tail. Pass through the ninth and 10th beads just strung (figure 1).

figure 1

Pull the thread tight, causing the beads to sit side by side. Pass through the next two beads in the strand and pull tight; repeat until all beads have been used. Pass through the first column of two A beads and through the final column to form a circle (figure 2).

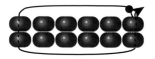

figure 2

*Rounds 1–23*: Use A beads to work tubular herringbone stitch off of the base ring for 23 rounds with six A beads in each round.

*Round 24*: Pick up two A beads, pass down through the next A bead of the previous round, pick up one A bead, and pass up through the next A bead of the previous round to form an increase; repeat around.

*Round 25*: Repeat round 24, this time adding two A beads between columns.

*Round 26*: Repeat round 24, this time adding three A beads between columns.

*Round 27*: Repeat round 24, this time adding two A beads, one D bead, and two A beads between columns.

*Round 28*: Repeat round 24, this time adding two A beads, passing through the nearest D bead of the previous round, and adding two more A beads between columns.

*Round 29*: Repeat round 24, this time adding three A beads, one D bead, and three A beads between columns (figure 3).

**figure 3**

Weave through beads to exit from an A bead in round 18. Pick up one C bead and pass through the next A bead on the column; repeat for all three columns. Weave through beads to exit from an A bead in round 11; in the same manner, add one C bead between columns (figure 4). Secure the thread and trim.

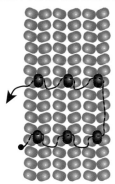

**figure 4**

## Rings

Use a single thread to pick up 18 B beads, leaving a short tail. Wrap the beads around the base between the round of C beads previously stitched, and tie a knot to form a tight circle; pass through the first B bead strung. Pick up one B, one D, and one B, then skip one B on the circle and pass through the next B; repeat eight times for a total of nine picots. Repeat the thread path to reinforce, making as many passes as possible (figure 5).

**figure 5**

Make two more rings, and place one above the second set of C beads and one above the flared end.

## Ear Wire

String one lochrose bead, one gray pearl, and the base (flared end first) onto a head pin. Use round-nose pliers to bend the head pin into a U shape just ¼ inch (6 mm) from where the head pin exits the base (figure 6).

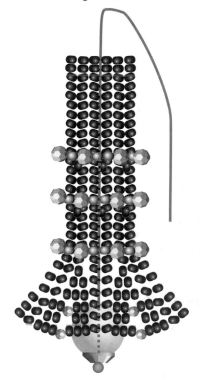

**figure 6**

Repeat all steps to make another earring.

**THE WAY IT MOVES**
Because the peyote-stitched rings are simply strung onto the base and left unmoored, they move around it.

## SUPPLIES

Silver size 15° seed beads, 2 g (A)

Dark gray charlottes, 4 g (B)

44 sapphire crystal rounds, 2 mm (C)

6 anodized aluminum jump rings,
¾ inch (1.9 cm) inner diameter,
1 inch (2.5 cm) outer diameter

2 silver earring posts with small pads

Thread

Wax

Needles

Scissors

Wire cutters

Chain-nose pliers, 2 pairs

Two-part jeweler's epoxy


## FINISHED SIZE

2 inches (5.1 cm) long


## TECHNIQUE

Right angle weave

# ROLLING LINKS EARRINGS

**Right angle weave covers anodized aluminum jump rings that interlock with one another, forming a pretty chain-like earring. The final touch is the tiny crystals that form a sparkling edge, adding glint and glimmer.**

## Jump Rings

Cut ¼ inch (6 mm) off of each end of one aluminum jump ring. Use both pairs of chain-nose pliers to grasp each end of the ring and carefully form it back into a circle. This is the top ring; set it aside. Repeat with another jump ring, but after re-forming it, insert the jaws of the chain-nose pliers into the jump ring's opening and open the pliers wide to reshape it into an oval. This is the center ring; set it aside. Wihout cutting it, reshape a third ring into an oval as you did with the center ring; this will be the bottom ring.

## Top Ring

1 Use single thread and B beads to bead a right-angle-weave strip 24 units long and four rows wide. Join the two short ends of the strip to form a ring, using a right-angle-weave thread path (figure 1).

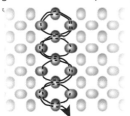

**figure 1**

### THE WAY IT MOVES
The links tumble, rock, and roll around each other.

2 Use the two-part epoxy to glue the flat face of one earring post to the back of the top ring, at the center top of the oval ring. Allow to dry.

3 Position the beaded ring on the inside diameter of the top jump ring, with the working thread exiting a B bead on the long edge. Pick up one B bead and pass through the opposite edge bead. Pick up one B bead and pass through the first edge bead, the bead just added, and the edge bead of the next unit. Pick up one B bead and pass through the opposite edge bead, the side bead of the previous connection unit, the original edge bead exited in this unit, the B bead just added, and the edge bead of the next unit; repeat until the join is complete, working around the earring post as necessary (figure 2).

**figure 2**

## Bottom Ring

Use single thread and B beads to make a strip of right angle weave 28 units long and four rows wide. Join the two short ends to form a beaded ring. Position the beaded ring on the inside diameter of the bottom jump ring and repeat the join as for the top ring, omitting the earring post.

## Center Ring

Use single thread and A beads to bead a strip of right angle weave 22 units long and three rows wide. Open the center jump ring, link it between the top and bottom rings, and close it. Position the strip of beading between the top and bottom rings and join the short ends together to form a beaded ring. Position the beaded ring on the inside diameter of the center jump ring and repeat the join as for the bottom ring, this time using C beads (figure 3).

**figure 3**

Repeat all steps to make a second earring.

# LAVENDER EARRINGS

Suspend crystal teardrops within oval frames of lavender cubic right angle weave. Contrasting beads—copper on one face as shown above, dark silver on the other— form a checkerboard design. The difference is subtle. Choose a different palette, and everyone will spot the difference.

## Base Strip

*Bottom*: Working with single thread, pick up three C beads and one D bead; tie an overhand knot. Weave through the beads to exit from the D bead. *Note*: These four beads form the bottom of the cube (figure 1).

**figure 1**

*Wall 1*: Pick up one C bead, one D bead, and one C bead. Pass through the last D bead exited and the next C bead on the bottom of the cube (figure 2).

**figure 2**

### THE WAY IT MOVES

These fun earrings gyrate beneath your lobes while the dangles shimmy to and fro. Wear them with the copper beads facing the front—or flip the frame on the ear wire to show off the dark silver beads instead.

*Wall 2*: Pick up two C beads; pass through the side C bead of the previous wall, the last bottom C bead exited, and the next bottom C bead (figure 3).

**figure 3**

*Wall 3*: Pick up two C beads; pass through the side C bead of the previous wall, the last bottom C bead exited, the next bottom C bead, and the side C bead of wall 1 (figure 4).

**figure 4**

*Wall 4*: Pick up one C bead; pass through the side C bead of wall 3, the last bottom C bead exited, the side C bead from wall 1, and the D bead at the top of wall 1 (figure 5).

**figure 5**

Continue working cubic right angle weave (figure 6), repeating walls 1 to 4 for a total of 29 units. *Note*: The tops of the walls just added become the bottom of your next cube.

**figure 6**

## SUPPLIES

Dark gray size 15° seed beads, 1 g (A)

Copper size 15° seed beads, 1 g (B)

Matte lavender size 11° seed beads, 5 g (C)

58 black diamond crystal round beads, 2 mm (D)

6 dark silver faceted metal heishi beads, 2 x 3 mm

2 golden shadow crystal teardrop beads, 12 x 8 mm

2 gunmetal ball-end head pins

6 inches (15.2 cm) of gunmetal wire, 22 gauge

2 gunmetal ear wires

Thread

Wax

Needles

Scissors

Wire cutters

Chain-nose pliers

Round-nose pliers

## FINISHED SIZE

Beadwork, 1 x 1½ inches (2.5 x 3.8 cm)

## TECHNIQUE

Cubic right angle weave

## Join the Ends

*Wall 1*: Weave through the beads to exit from a D bead at the top of the final unit. Position the other end of the strip so a D bead is directly opposite the one you're exiting. Pick up one C bead; pass through the corresponding D bead. Pick up one C bead; pass through the last D bead exited at the other end of the strip, and continue through to the next C bead on the top of the next wall (figure 7).

**figure 7**

*Wall 2*: Pick up one C bead; pass through the next bottom bead at the other side of the strip, then continue to weave through beads to exit from the next top bead (figure 8).

**figure 8**

*Wall 3*: Repeat wall 2.

*Wall 4*: All four beads are already in position, so just work a thread path of right angle weave to secure (figure 9). Weave through the beads to exit from an outside edge C bead on one side of the nearest D bead.

**figure 9**

## Embellish

Pick up one A bead and pass through the next outside edge C bead; repeat around for a total of 30 beads. Weave through the beads to exit from the inside edge and repeat (figure 10).

**figure 10**

Weave through the beads to exit from the outside edge at the other side of the oval. Pick up one B bead and pass through the next C bead; repeat around for a total of 30 beads. Weave through beads to exit from the inside edge. Repeat (figure 11). Secure the thread and trim. Set the oval aside.

**figure 11**

## Wire Wrap

On a head pin, slide on one metal heishi bead, one crystal teardrop bead, and one metal heishi bead. Form a wrapped loop to secure the beads, creating a bead dangle. Cut a 3-inch (7.6 cm) piece of wire; form a wrapped loop on one end that attaches to the wrapped loop on the bead dangle.

Pass the wire up through the center of the top cube structure from the underside. String one heishi on the wire and form another wrapped loop (figure 12). Attach an ear wire.

**figure 12**

Repeat all steps to make a second earring.

# GABRIELLA RING

This bold ring will be a certain conversation-starter. It begins with a right angle woven circle filled with a beautiful crystal rondelle. The embellished band is comfortable to wear.

## SUPPLIES

Light gray size 15° seed beads, 1 g (A)

Beige-lined size 15° seed beads, 1 g (B)

Dark gray size 15° seed beads, 1 g (C)

Beige-lined size 11° seed beads, 1 g (D)

14 platinum crystal pearl round beads, 3 mm (E)

14 platinum crystal pearl round beads, 4 mm (F)

14 light metallic gold crystal round beads, 2 mm (G)

1 dark gray crystal rondelle, 18 mm

1 sand opal crystal lochrose bead, 4 mm

Thread

Wax

Needles

Scissors

## FINISHED SIZE

Ring top, 1¼ inches (3.2 cm) across

## TECHNIQUES

Peyote stitch

Right angle weave

**THE WAY IT MOVES**
The top of the ring twirls around its sparkling center.

## Ring Top

*Round 1*: Thread 72 inches (1.8 m) of thread and double it. Pull one end of the thread so you have a 12-inch (30.5 cm) length of single thread. Pick up four A beads and position them 4 inches (10.2 cm) from the end of the doubled thread; tie a double overhand knot. *Note*: The single tail thread will be used to complete rounds of peyote stitch later in the process.

Complete 13 units of right angle weave and join the last unit to the first so you have a ring with a total of 14 units. Exit from a top A bead.

*Round 2*: Work a round of tubular right angle weave using one A bead for each side and one D bead for the top of each unit. Exit from a top D bead.

*Round 3*: Still in tubular right angle weave, work a round using D beads. Exit from a top D bead.

*Round 4*: Continue in tubular right angle weave, using one E bead and one D bead for each side and one F bead for the top of each unit (figure 1).

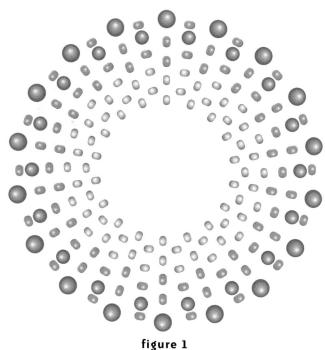

**figure 1**

*Round 5*: Weave through beads to exit from an D bead at the top of round 3. Pick up one D bead and pass through the next E bead; repeat around. Pass through the first D bead added.

*Round 6*: Pick up one F bead and pass through the next D bead; repeat around. Secure the thread and trim (figure 2).

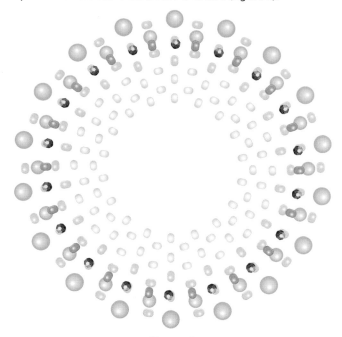

**figure 2**

*Round 7 (back)*: Follow along with figure 3. Weave the tail thread through beads to exit from a bottom A bead of round 1. Pick up one A bead and pass through the next two A beads of round 1; repeat around and step up through the first bead added in this round.

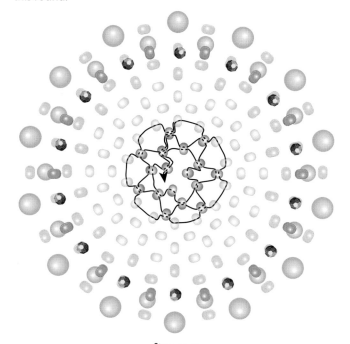

**figure 3**

*Round 8 (back)*: Pick up one A bead and pass through the next A bead of round 7; repeat around for a total of seven beads. Step up through the first bead added in this round.

**Round 9 (back)**: Pick up one A bead and pass through the next two A beads twice. Pick up one A bead and pass through the next three A beads. Pull gently to tighten. Secure the thread and trim. Set aside.

## Ring Band

**Base**: Use single thread and B beads to make a band of right angle weave four units wide and as long as necessary to fit your finger. **Note**: Twenty-nine units make a size 8 ring. Join the short ends to form a tube (figure 4).

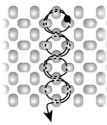

**figure 4**

**Round 1**: Weave through beads to exit from a B bead on the edge. Pick up one C bead and pass through the next B bead; repeat around.

**Rounds 2–4**: Weave through beads to exit from a B bead on the next base row. Add one C bead between each B bead as before, but skip four units in the center of the round. Repeat to embellish each round, leaving the center empty to add the medallion later.

**Round 5**: Repeat round 1 to embellish the other edge of the base (figure 5).

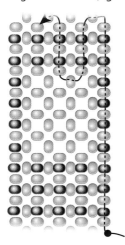

**figure 5**

**Round 6**: Weave through beads to exit from a C bead along the edge of the base. Pick up one D bead and pass through the nearest C bead of the next round. Pick up one D bead and pass through the first C bead exited, the first D bead just added, the second C bead entered, the second D bead just added, and the next C bead along the edge (figure 6).

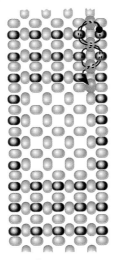

**figure 6**

Repeat to add D beads between all C beads at each edge of the base except the three center units (figure 7). Secure the thread and trim.

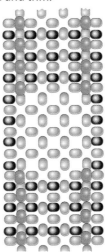

**figure 7**

## Assemble

**1** Attach a new double thread that exits from the middle B bead of the four units that were left unembellished. Pass

through the center of the medallion. Pick up the rondelle, the lochrose bead, and one C bead. Pass back through the lochrose bead, the rondelle, and the medallion, then pass through adjacent beads on the base (figures 8 and 9).

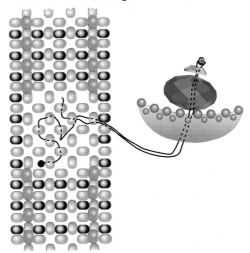

**figure 8**

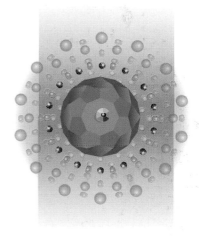

**figure 9**

**2** Repeat the thread path to reinforce. Secure the thread and trim.

**3** Use double thread to pick up 12 D beads. Wrap the strand between the ring top and the ring band and tie a knot with the working and tail threads to form a ring. Pass through all the D beads several times to reinforce. Secure the thread and trim. **Note**: This ring of beads is used to stabilize the piece of jewelry when it's worn.

Bronze size 15° seed beads, 1 g (A)

Tan-lined clear size 11° seed beads, 1 g (B)

Silver-lined opal size 11° seed beads, 1 g (C)

Matte light sea foam size 8° seed beads, 2 g (D)

20 jet AB2X crystal bicones, 3 mm (E)

113 light metallic gold crystal bicones, 3 mm (F)

10 platinum crystal pearl rounds, 3 mm (G)

1 clear AB crystal rivoli, 14 mm

Thread

Wax

Needles

Scissors

## FINISHED SIZE

Ring top, 1½ inches (3.8 cm) across

## TECHNIQUES

Ladder stitch

Right angle weave

# REVOLUTION RING

This ring combines two separate elements. The band and its top are one piece, and you'll use a unique ladder stitch technique to make the lacy spinner. Simply pull the ring band through the center of the spinner to wear them together. You can make a whole host of interchangeable spinners in different colors.

## Spinner

**1** Using doubled and waxed thread, pick up one D bead, and then pass through it again and pull it to 8 inches (20.3 cm) from the end to form a stop bead. Pick up four D beads. Pick up the following sequence nine times: three B beads and eight D beads, for a total of 99 beads strung. Pick up three B beads and four D beads so you have ten groups of B beads on the thread, beginning and ending with a group of four D beads. Don't push the beads all the way to the stop bead; leave some slack in the thread. Pass through the 11th, 10th, ninth, eighth, and seventh bead from the end of the strand (four D beads and one B bead), as shown in figure 1.

**figure 1**

**2** Pull tightly and the beads will align themselves into two columns of D beads with three B beads on the top of the double column. Pick up five B beads, skip the middle B bead previously added, and then pass down through the next B bead and the following four D beads. Pass up through the four D beads in the adjacent column (figure 2).

**figure 2**

**3** Pick up one G bead and pass up through the next four D beads on the strand (figure 3).

**figure 3**

**4** Pass up through the next four D beads and one B bead on the strand (figure 4).

**figure 4**

**5** Continue alternating between steps 2, 3, and 4 until you have 10 spokes. Pass up through the first column of D beads. Pick up one G bead and pass through the final column of D beads and back up through the first coulmn (figure 5).

**figure 5**

## THE WAY IT MOVES

The band and its top are bicone heaven, with a crystal rivoli held inside a bezel setting. The spinner turns easily around the ring, and it sways and flops gently like an anemone caught in sea currents. You embellish just one side of it with crystals so you can wear the ring two different ways—three if you opt for no spinner.

**6** Weave through all of the D beads to reinforce. Exit up through a top D bead in the right column of one of the spokes (figure 6).

**figure 6**

**7** *Pick up one A bead, one E bead, and one A bead, and pass through the tip B bead of the spoke. Pick up one A bead, one E bead, and one A bead. Pass down through the top D bead in the left column of the spoke, through the nearest G bead, and up through the top D bead in the right column of the next spoke. Repeat from * nine times (figure 7). Weave in the thread and trim.

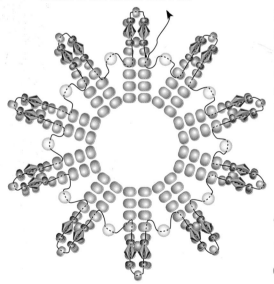

**figure 7**

## Ring

**8** Use double thread and F beads to create a strip of right angle weave 11 units long and two rows wide. Join the two short ends to form a circle (figure 8).

**figure 8**

**9** Pass through all of the edge beads of the current row twice and pull tightly. Weave to the edge beads of the first row. *Note:* This will form a cup for your rivoli (figure 9).

**figure 9**

**10** Place the rivoli into the beadwork face up. Pass through all beads on the top edge twice and pull tightly. *Weave to exit the middle row of beads on the edge of the rivoli. Pick up one C bead and pass through the next F bead. Repeat from * 11 times, for a total of 12 C beads (figure 10).

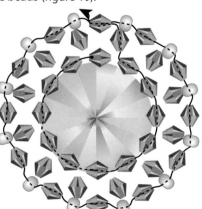

**figure 10**

**11** Weave through beads to exit from an edge F bead beneath the rivoli. Use F beads to stitch a strip of right angle weave off of the edge that is one row wide and 13 units long, or long enough to fit around your finger. Join the end of the strip to an edge F bead directly opposite from the start bead (figure 11).

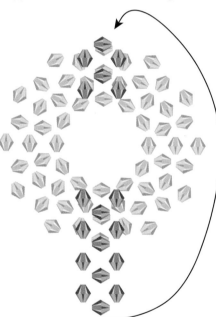

**figure 11**

Thread the ring band through the hole of the spinner.

Of course, you can wear the ring without the spinner, or make several colors and change them at will!

# Chapter 4

# BRACELETS

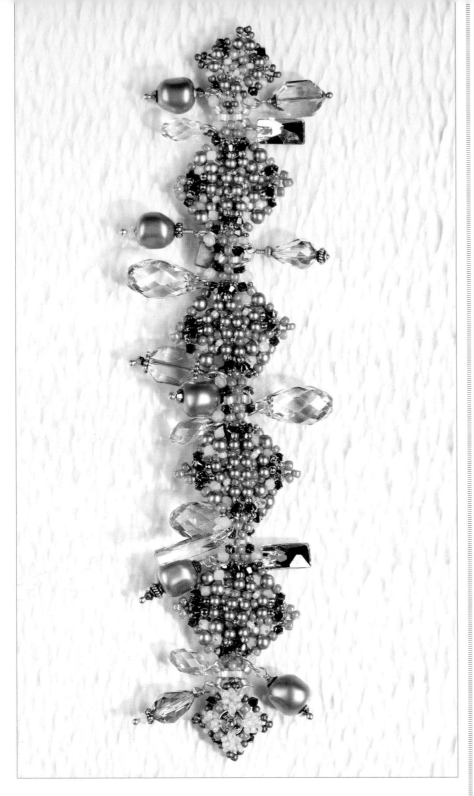

# CHARMING BRACELET

This bracelet—both elegant and fun—starts with four diamond medallions embellished with seed beads and crystals. Two smaller diamonds serve to hide the snap clasp. When all the diamonds are stitched corner to corner, the spaces between are the perfect place for adding crystal and pearl dangles.

Gray luster size 15° seed beads, 1 g (A)

Gray luster size 11° seed beads, 1 g (B)

Gray matte size 11° seed beads, 1 g (C)

White luster size 11° seed beads, 1 g (D)

Gray luster size 8° seed beads, 7 g (E)

White luster size 8° seed beads, 1 g (F)

84 light metallic gold crystal bicones, 3 mm (G)

34 white opal AB crystal bicones, 3 mm (H)

20 white opal fire-polished rounds, 3 mm (I)

56 platinum crystal pearl rounds, 3 mm (J)

32 platinum crystal pearl rounds, 4 mm (K)

2 silver shade crystal graphic beads, 18 mm

2 clear AB crystal teardrops, 12 x 8 mm

3 clear briolette pendants, 11 x 5.5 mm

3 clear briolette pendants, 17 x 8.5 mm

5 platinum baroque crystal pearls, 12 mm

3 clear foil-back crystal rectangles, 12.5 x 7 mm

1 silver shade crystal rhombus, 14 mm

1 silver shade crystal column pendant, 20 mm

7 light gold metallic crystal lochrose beads, 4 mm

9 assorted silver metal spacer beads, 3 to 5 mm

20 silver jump rings, 6 mm

9 sterling silver ball-end head pins, 22 gauge

1 silver snap, 7 mm (size 3)

Thread

Wax

Needles

Scissors

Wire cutters

Round-nose pliers

Chain-nose pliers

**FINISHED SIZE**

7¼ inches (18.4 cm) long

**TECHNIQUE**

Ladder stitch

**THE WAY IT MOVES**
Pretty dangles twinkle, shimmer, and click together as you move your wrist.

## Large Medallion Base

*Round 1:* Using double thread, pick up eight E beads, leaving a 6-inch (15.2 cm) tail. Pass through the seventh bead strung (figure 1) and pull tight so the beads sit next to one another.

**figure 1**

Pass through the next bead (figure 2) and pull tight to align it next to the other ladder-stitched beads. Repeat to form a ladder-stitched strip.

**figure 2**

With the thread exiting up from the top of the final bead added, pass down through the first bead of the strip and up through the final bead to form a ring (figure 3).

**figure 3**

*Round 2:* Pick up three E beads, and then pass down through the next round 1 bead and up through the next bead. Repeat three times for a total of four points. Exit through the first bead added in this round (figure 4).

**figure 4**

*Round 3:* Pick up five E beads and pass through the third bead added in this point of round 2. Pick up one K bead and pass through the first E bead of the next point. Repeat three times for a total of four points. Weave through beads to

exit from the third E bead added in this round (figure 5).

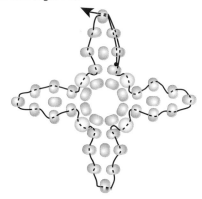

**figure 5**

*Round 4:* Pick up three E beads and pass through the last bead exited to form a picot. Pass through the next three E beads of the point, the K bead, and the first four E beads of the next point. Repeat three times for a total of four picots (figure 6).

**figure 6**

## Large Medallion Embellishment

*Inner cross:* Pick up one B bead, one G bead, one B bead, and one J bead; pass down through the nearest E bead of round 1 at the base of the point. Pick up one J bead and pass up through the next E bead of round 1. *Note:* This completes the first half of the first point and turns the corner to the next point. The turning pearls have a tendency to fall into the middle, but don't worry, they will align properly in a future step.

*Pick up one J bead, one B bead, one G bead, and one B bead; pass through the middle E bead of the next point added in round 3. Pick up one B bead, one G bead, one B bead, and one J bead; pass through the nearest E bead of round 1 at the base of the point. Pick up one J bead and pass up through the next E bead of round 1. Repeat from * to embellish the next two points and the second half of the first point, exiting from the middle E bead of round 3 in the first point (figure 7).

**figure 7**

*Sides:* Pick up one B bead, one G bead, one E bead, one K bead, one E bead, one G bead, and one B bead; pass through the middle E bead of round 3 in the next point. Repeat three times to connect all the points. Weave through beads to exit from the first K added in this section (figure 8).

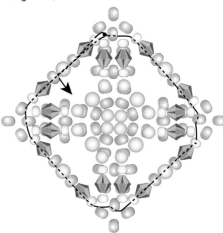

**figure 8**

*Outer cross:* Pick up one H bead and pass through the nearest K bead added in round 3. Pick up one H bead and pass through the K bead previously exited. Weave through beads to exit the next K bead added in the sides. Repeat twice, then repeat once, this time weaving through beads to exit from a J bead at the center of the medallion (figure 9).

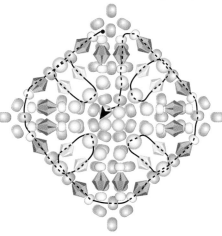

**figure 9**

*Center:* Pick up one A bead and pass through the next J bead; repeat three times (figure 10). Secure the thread and trim. Set the medallion aside.

**figure 10**

Repeat all the steps above three more times to make a total of four large embellished medallions.

## Clasp Top

Repeat the large medallion with these adjustments:

*Round 1:* Use D beads.

*Round 2:* Use D beads.

*Round 3:* Use D beads for the points and E beads between the points.

*Round 4:* Use C beads.

*Inner cross:* Use one A bead, one J bead, and one A bead. Use one E bead in the center.

*Sides:* Use one D bead, one B bead, one G bead, one B bead, and one D bead.

*Outer cross:* Skip.

*Center:* Use one D bead between the center E beads.

Neatly stitch the male half of the snap to the exact center of the underside of this medallion.

## Clasp Bottom

Repeat only rounds 1–4 and the sides of the Clasp Top. Neatly stitch the female half of the snap to the top of this medallion so it matches the clasp top.

## Assemble

*Join large medallions:* Start a new double thread that exits from the middle E bead of a picot added in round 4 of one of the large medallions. Pick up one F bead and pass through the middle E bead of a corresponding picot on a second medallion. Pick up one F bead and pass through the last E bead exited on the first medallion and the first F bead just added. Pick up one G bead, one I bead, and one A bead; pass through the nearest G and B beads on the side of the second medallion, the middle of the five E beads added in round 3, and the B and G beads on the other side of the same medallion. Pick up one A bead, one I bead, and one G bead; pass through the second F bead added in this section. Repeat the same sequence to complete the second side of the join (the thread path is shown on the left side of figure 11).

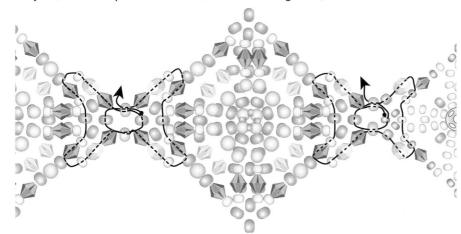

**figure 11**

*Join small medallions:* Complete the same thread path as the join for the large medallions, but use one F bead and one I bead for the connections. On the small medallion side of the join, pass through C and D side beads (figure 11, the thread path on the right side of the illustration).

*Dangles:* Use one head pin to string one metal spacer, one crystal element, and one metal spacer; form a wrapped loop to secure the beads. Use one jump ring to connect the dangle to the space between the medallions, as shown in figure 12.

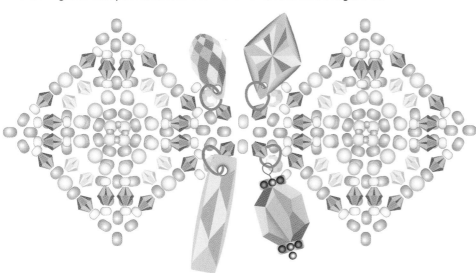

**figure 12**

Use one jump ring to connect a horizontally drilled bead to the area across from where the previous dangle was just placed. Use the remaining materials to make dangles and attach them to the bracelet, with four placed between each medallion (figure 13).

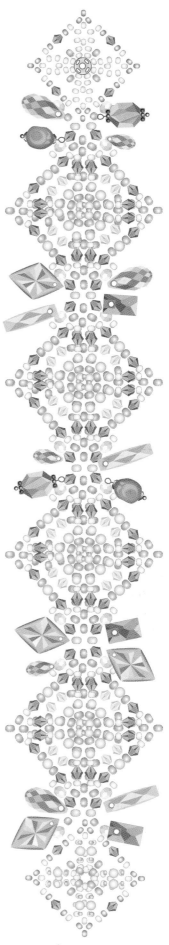

**figure 13**

Bronze size 15° seed beads, 1 g (A)

Black size 15° seed beads, 1 g (B)

Bronze size 11° seed beads, 4 g (C)

Green size 11° seed beads, 4 g (D)

Bronze size 8° seed beads, 3 g (E)

Black size 8° seed beads, 3 g (F)

136 jet crystal bicones, 3 mm (G)

12 dorado crystal bicones, 3 mm (H)

15 olivine crystal bicones, 4 mm (I)

6 gold crystal pearl round beads,
3 mm (J)

16 gold fire-polished round beads,
4 mm (K)

2 snaps, ¼ inch (6 mm)

Thread

Wax

Needles

Scissors

## FINISHED SIZE

6¾ inches (17.1 cm) long

## TECHNIQUES

Ladder stitch

Diamond stitch

# CAROUSEL BRACELET

Create a lacy band of crystal-encrusted, diamond-shaped segments. Form a right-angle-weave medallion with a sparkling spinner on top. Combine both, and shazam! You've got a bracelet with some major bling.

## Band

**Row 1, top unit, round 1:** Use a double thread to pick up three D beads and one G bead; repeat three times for a total of four groups (figure 1). Tie a square knot to form a circle. Pass through the first three D beads and one G bead.

**figure 1**

### THE WAY IT MOVES
You can rotate the spinner around and around on the focal element.

**Row 1, top unit, round 2:** Pick up one C bead and pass through the next G bead; repeat three times, pulling tight after each pass (figure 2). Pass through the first C bead.

**figure 2**

**Row 1, top unit, round 3:** Pick up three B beads and pass through the next C bead; repeat three times (figure 3). Pass though the first and second B beads.

**figure 3**

**Row 1, top unit, round 4:** Pick up one C bead and pass through the middle B bead in the next group; repeat three times (figure 4). Weave through beads to exit from a middle D bead in one of the groups of round 1. **Note:** This is a shared bead.

**figure 4**

**Row 1, bottom unit, round 1:** Pick up one D bead, one G bead, three D beads, and one G bead; repeat twice. Pick up one D bead and pass through the shared D bead to close the circle (figure 5).

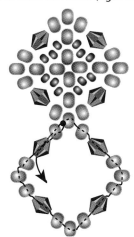

**figure 5**

**Row 1, bottom unit, rounds 2–4:** Repeat row 1, top unit, rounds 2–4. Weave through beads to exit from the middle D bead of the group on the right side of round 1 of this unit.

**Row 2, bottom unit:** Repeat row 1, top unit, all rounds, this time exiting through the middle D of the top group of round 1 (figure 6).

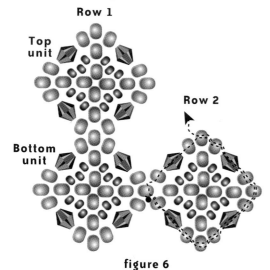

**Row 1**

**Top unit**

**Row 2**

**Bottom unit**

**figure 6**

**Row 2, top unit, round 1:** Pick up one D bead, one G bead, and one D bead. Pass through the middle D on the right side group of round 1 of the top unit of row 1. Pick up one D bead. Pick up one G bead and three D beads twice. Pick up one G bead and one D bead. Pass through the last D exited in the bottom unit of this row and the first D bead and G bead added in this round (figure 7).

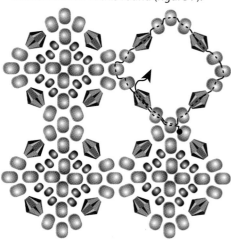

**figure 7**

**Row 2, top unit, rounds 2–4:** Repeat row 1, top unit, exiting through the middle D bead of the group on the right side of round 1 of this unit.

**Rows 3–7:** Repeat row 2, all rounds, five times.

**Rows 8–10:** Repeat row 2 three times, this time only working round 1 of each unit. This is where the spinner will be attached.

**Rows 11–16:** Repeat row 2, all rounds, six times.

**Row 17:** Repeat row 2, this time only working round 1 of each unit. This is where the snaps will be sewn.

**Snaps:** Securely sew the male side of one snap to the face of each unit of row 17. Secure the thread and trim. Start a new thread that exits from row 1. Sew the female side of one snap to the back of each unit of row 1 (figure 8).

**Center:** Weave through beads to exit from a shared D bead between the two units of row 1. Pick up one B bead, one C bead, one K bead, one C bead, and one B bead, then pass through the shared D bead of the next row (figure 9); repeat for a total of 16 groups. Secure the thread and trim. Set the band aside.

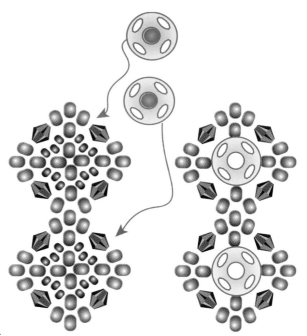

**figure 8**

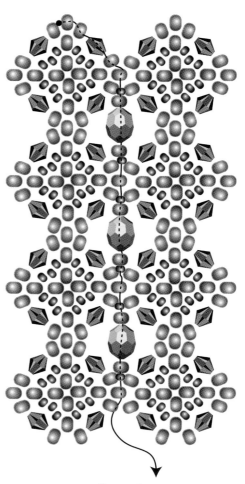

**figure 9**

## Post

**1** Add a stop bead to the end of a length of waxed double thread, leaving an 8-inch (20.3 cm) tail. Pick up 36 F beads and pass through the 31st, 32nd, and 33rd beads (figure 10). Pull tightly to align the beads in a column three beads high.

**figure 10**

**2** Pass through the next three beads (figure 11).

**figure 11**

**3** Continue until all of the beads have been used and there are 12 columns. Exiting from the top of the last column, pass through the top of the first column and back through the last column to form a ring (figure 12).

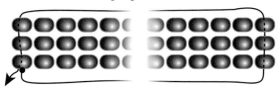

**figure 12**

**4** Pick up three D beads and pass down through all three F beads in the next column to form a picot at the top of the ring, then pick up three F beads and pass up through the three F beads in the next column to form a picot at the bottom of the ring. Repeat for all of the columns (figure 13).

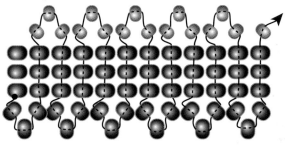

**figure 13**

**5** Weave through the beads to exit from the first F bead of one of the bottom picots just added. Pick up five F beads, skip the middle F bead of the picot, and pass through the next F bead. Pick up one I bead and pass through the first bead of the next F picot. Repeat five times to connect all six F picots, forming spokes (figure 14).

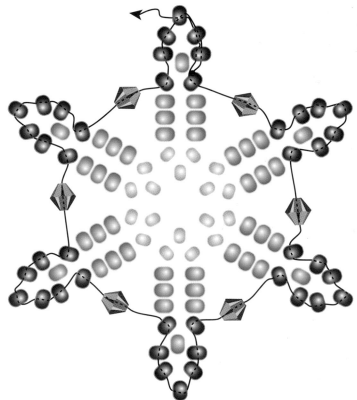

**figure 14**

**6** Weave through the beads to exit from the middle bead of the first spoke. Pick up three E beads and pass though the last F bead exited to form a picot. Pick up one C bead, one H bead, one C bead, one I bead, one C bead, one H bead, and one C bead; pass through the middle of the five F beads in the next spoke. Repeat five times to connect all six spokes (figure 15).

**7** Weave through the beads to exit through a middle D bead of one of the picots at the other edge of the initial ring. Pick up one C bead and pass through the middle D bead of the next picot; repeat five times to connect all six D picots. Step up through the first C added. Work one more round of circular peyote stitch with one B bead in each stitch. Weave through beads to exit from the first edge F bead of the nearest spoke.

**8** *Pick up one J bead and one A bead; pass back through the J bead and the F bead in the adjacent column so the fringe sits below a D picot. Weave through beads to exit from the first F bead of the next spoke. Repeat from * to add one fringe to each spoke (figure 16). Don't trim the thread; set the post aside.

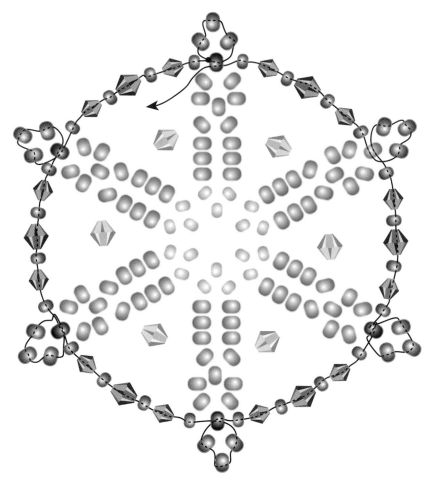

**figure 15**

**figure 16**

58

## Spinner

**9** Add a stop bead to the end of a length of waxed double thread, leaving an 8-inch (20.3 cm) tail. Pick up three E beads. Pick up the following eight times: three D beads and six E beads. Then pick up three D beads and three E beads. Pass through the ninth, eighth, seventh, and sixth beads from the end (three E beads and one D bead), as shown in figure 17.

**10** Pull tightly so the beads align themselves into two columns of E beads with three D beads on the top of the column (a picot). Pick up five D beads, skip the middle D bead of the picot just formed, and pass down through the next D bead and the adjacent three E beads. Pass up through the three E beads in the adjacent column (figure 18).

**11** Pick up one I bead and pass through the next three E beads of the initial strand (figure 19).

**12** Pass through the next three E beads and one D bead (figure 20).

**figure 17**

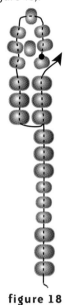

**figure 18**

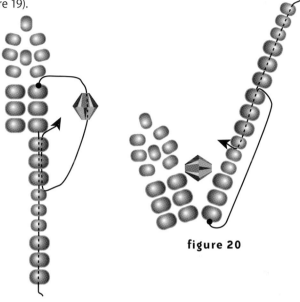

**figure 19**

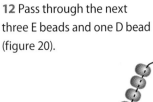

**figure 20**

**13** Repeat steps 10, 11 and 12 until all nine spokes have tips. Do not join. Weave through all of the columns of E beads to reinforce (figure 21).

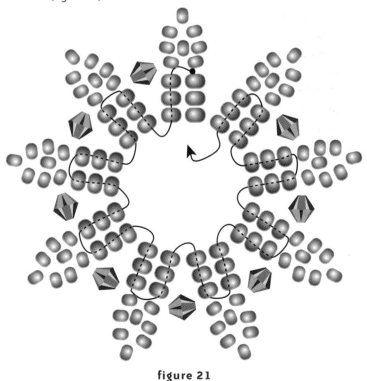

**figure 21**

**14** Place the spinner underneath the pearls on the post and join the first and last columns by adding one I bead between them.

## SUPPLIES

Transparent green size 15° seed beads, 1 g (A)

Silver size 11° seed beads, 6 g (B)

Green brown iris size 11° seed beads, 14 g (C)

36 platinum crystal pearl round beads, 3 mm (D)

18 platinum crystal pearl round beads, 4 mm (E)

24 olivine crystal round beads, 2 mm (F)

24 olivine crystal bicones, 3 mm (G)

6 dark silver metal spacer beads, 2 x 6 mm (H)

1 gunmetal rectangular magnetic two-strand clasp, 10 x 22 mm

Thread

Wax

Needles

Scissors

## FINISHED SIZE

7½ inches (19.1 cm) long

## TECHNIQUES

Peyote stitch

Cubic right angle weave

Right angle weave

# VICTORIAN SLIDE BRACELET

**Pretty pearl- and crystal-encrusted beaded beads move freely along a cubic right-angle-weave strap, evoking a gracious Victorian slide bracelet.**

## Large Beaded Bead

*Base:* Use a single thread and B beads to create a strip of right angle weave seven units wide and 13 units long. Join the short sides to form a circle (figure 1). Exit from an edge B bead.

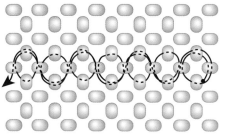

**figure 1**

*Layer 1:* Pick up one A bead and pass through the next edge B bead; repeat around for a total of 14 A beads. Weave through the beads to exit from a B bead in the next vertical row. Pick up one C bead and pass through the next B bead; repeat four more times for a total of five C beads. Pass through the horizontal B bead and the nearest B bead in the next vertical row. Place a C bead in each of the next five spaces, turn, and repeat for the next row. Repeat three times for a total of six rows of five C beads each. Weave through beads to exit from an edge

B bead. Pick up one A bead and pass through the next B bead; repeat around for a total of 14 A beads. Weave through beads to exit from the upper left corner C bead in the sixth C-bead embellishment row (figure 2).

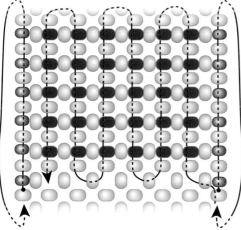

**figure 2**

*Layer 2:* Work in right angle weave, using the top row of C beads in layer 1 as side beads, D beads for the top and bottom of the first unit, G beads for the top and bottom of the second unit, E beads for the top and bottom of the third unit, G beads for the top and bottom of the fourth unit, and D beads for the top and bottom of the fifth unit (figure 3).

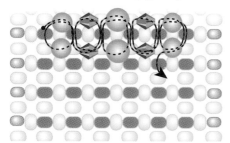

**figure 3**

Continue to make right-angle-weave units off of layer 1 in the same order as the first row. *Note:* You will only be adding the bottom beads of these units.

*Fringe:* Weave through beads to exit from a middle B bead one row past the embellishment rows. Pick up one H bead and one A bead; pass back through the H bead and the B bead originally exited to form a fringe (figure 4). Repeat the thread path to reinforce; secure this thread and trim. Start a new thread on the middle B bead on the opposite side of the ring and repeat to add a second fringe. Set aside.

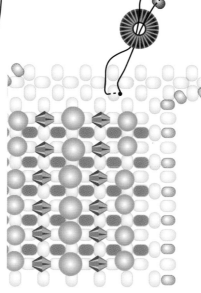

**figure 4**

## Medium Beaded Bead

*Base:* Using a single thread and B beads, make a strip of right angle weave five units wide and 13 units long. Join the ends into a circle.

*Layer 1:* Place A edge beads and C middle row beads as with the large beaded bead, but add only four rows of C beads. Weave through beads to exit from the upper left corner C bead.

*Layer 2:* Work in right angle weave, using the top row of C beads in layer 1 as side beads, D beads for the top and bottom of the first unit, E beads for the top and bottom of the second unit, and D beads for the top and bottom of the third unit (figure 5).

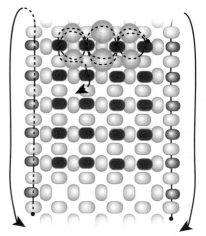

**figure 5**

Continue to work right-angle-weave units off of layer 1 in the same order as the first row. *Note:* You will only be adding the bottom beads of these units.

## THE WAY IT MOVES
You can position the sliders anywhere along the band—with space between each, some side by side with others apart, or all pushed together. The choice is yours.

*Layer 3:* Weave through beads to exit from the bottom right corner edge C bead of layer 1. Pick up one F bead and pass up through the next C bead; repeat five times for a total of six F beads. Pass through a B bead on the base. Pick up one A bead and pass through the next B bead to the left; repeat once. Pick up one F bead and pass down through the next C bead; repeat five times. Pass through a B bead on the base. Pick up one A bead and pass through the next B bead to the right; repeat once. Weave through beads to exit from the first F bead added in this layer. Pass through the next D bead. Pick up one A bead and pass through the nearest E bead. Pick up one A bead and pass through the following D bead and the nearest F bead to turn. Continue, adding A beads between the D and E beads and turning through F beads (figure 6).

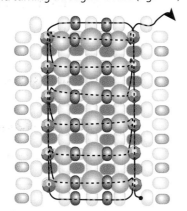

**figure 6**

*Fringe:* Repeat the fringe section from the large beaded bead. Secure the thread and trim. Set aside.

Make a second medium beaded bead.

## Small Beaded Bead

*Base:* Use a single thread and B beads to make a strip of right angle weave that's three units wide and 13 units long. Join the ends into a circle.

*Layer 1:* Place A edge beads and C middle row beads as in the large beaded bead, but add only two rows of C beads. Weave through the beads to exit from the upper left corner C bead.

*Layer 2:* Continue to work right angle weave, using the C beads in layer 1 as side beads and G beads for the top and bottom of each unit (figure 7). Secure the thread and trim it. Set the work aside.

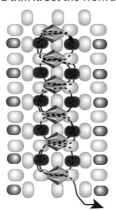

**figure 7**

Make a second small beaded bead.

## Band

**1** Use C beads to stitch a band of cubic right angle weave that's three cubes wide and 55 cubes long (figure 8). *Note:* This forms a bracelet 7½ inches (19.1 cm) long, including the width of the clasp; make more or fewer cubes to adjust.

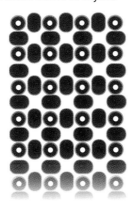

**figure 8**

**2** Slide a medium beaded bead, a small beaded bead, the large beaded bead, a small beaded bead, and a medium beaded bead onto the band.

## Clasp

**3** Determine the loop placement on the clasp and weave through beads to exit from an opposite bead on the end of the base. Pick up four A beads, pass through the loop on the clasp, then pass back through the last base bead exited and the next base end bead. Repeat to secure the second loop (figure 9).

**figure 9**

**4** Weave through beads to exit from an edge C bead. Pick up one A bead and pass through the next C bead; repeat around and step up through the first A bead just added. Use A beads to work tubular peyote stitch for one or two rounds as required to hide the clasp connection (figure 10).

**figure 10**

**5** Repeat steps 3 and 4 to finish the other end of the bracelet.

# PEANUT SLIDER BRACELET

Heavy beaded beads in subtly different colorways tumble between bands of peanut beads in this chunky cuff. With a wonderfully elegant closure mechanism, the ends of the bands abut, so there's no gap between the ends of the beadwork.

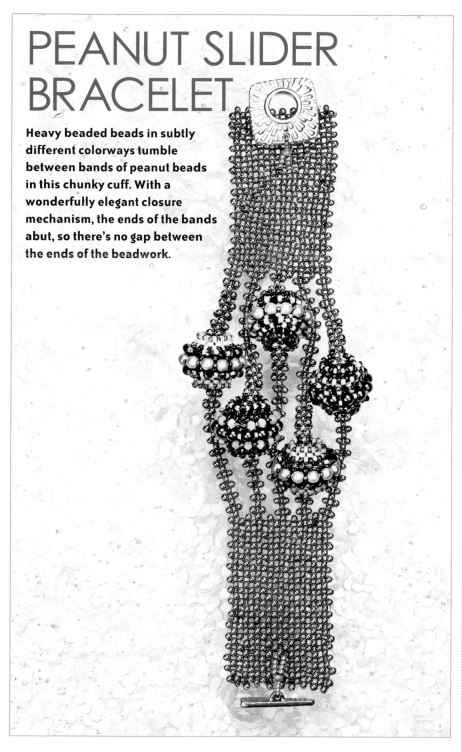

## SUPPLIES

Dark silver size 15° seed beads, 1 g (A)

Dark blue size 15° seed beads, 1 g (B)

Light gray size 15° seed beads, 1 g (C)

Light gray size 11° seed beads, 5 g (D)

Metallic dark blue size 11° seed beads, 3 g (E)

Brown iris size 11° seed beads, 3 g (F)

Silver size 11° peanut beads, 2 x 4 mm, 40 g (G)

2 light gray size 8° seed beads (H)

36 platinum crystal pearl round beads, 3 mm (I)

24 dark blue crystal pearl round beads, 3 mm (J)

24 sand opal crystal bicones, 3 mm (K)

72 metallic blue crystal bicones, 3 mm (L)

24 metallic light gold crystal bicones, 3 mm (M)

1 silver square decorative toggle clasp, 22 mm

Thread

Wax

Needles

Scissors

## FINISHED SIZE

7 inches (17.8 cm) long

## TECHNIQUE

Right angle weave

## THE WAY IT MOVES

The beaded beads whirl on their own axes. You can slide them along the narrow strands as if they were beads on an abacus.

## Beaded Bead 1

Use double thread and D beads to make a strip of right angle weave five units wide and 11 rows high. Stitch the first and last rows together to form a ring that's 12 rows around (figure 1).

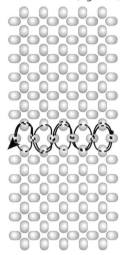

**figure 1**

*Layer 1:* Weave through beads to exit from a D bead at the edge of the ring. Pick up one A bead and pass through the next D bead to create a column of A beads; repeat around for a total of 12 A beads. Weave through beads to exit from a D bead in the second column. Pick up one F bead and pass through the next D bead; repeat around for a total of 12 F beads. Repeat for columns 3–5. For column 6, repeat column 1 (figure 2).

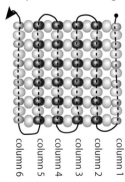

**figure 2**

*Layer 2:* Weave through beads to exit from an F bead in column 5. Use F beads to stitch right-angle-weave units on top

of layer 1 using the D beads added in layer 1 as the side beads (figure 3).

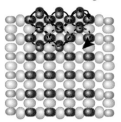

**figure 3**

*Layer 3:* Weave through beads to exit from an F bead added in layer 2. *Pick up one E bead and pass through the nearest F bead; repeat once. Pass through two F beads to turn. Repeat from * to embellish all rows (figure 4).

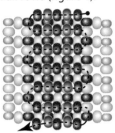

**figure 4**

*Layer 4:* Weave through beads to exit from an E bead added in layer 3, toward the edge. Work right-angle-weave units off of the top and bottom E beads added in layer 3, adding L beads for the outside edges of each unit and I beads for the center of each unit (figure 5).

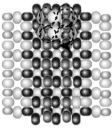

**figure 5**

*Layer 5:* Weave through beads to exit from an L bead added in layer 4. Pick up one A bead and pass through the next L bead; repeat around the ring. Weave through beads to exit from an I bead added in layer 4. Pick up one B bead and pass through the next I bead; repeat around. Weave through beads to exit from an L bead in the next column. Pick up one A bead and pass through the

next L bead; repeat around (figure 6). Secure the thread and trim.

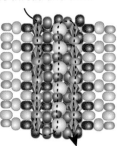

**figure 6**

Complete a second identical beaded bead.

## Beaded Bead 2

Repeat the pattern for beaded bead 1, but use E beads for the base; C and D beads for layer 1; D beads for layer 2; D beads for layer 3; M and J beads for layer 4; and A and C beads for layer 5 (figure 7).

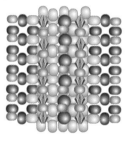

**figure 7**

## Beaded Bead 3

Repeat the pattern for beaded bead 1, with the following changes: use F beads for the base; C and E beads for layer 1; E beads for layer 2; E beads for layer 3; K and J beads for layer 4; and A and C beads for layer 5 (figure 8).

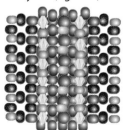

**figure 8**

## Beaded Bead 4

Repeat the pattern for beaded bead 1, this time using F beads for the base; A and D beads for layer 1; D beads for layer 2; D beads for layer 3; L and I beads for layer 4; and C and B beads for layer 5 (figure 9).

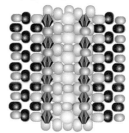

**figure 9**

## Base

*Strips:* Use double thread and G beads to create a strip of right angle weave nine units wide and 14 units long. Don't trim the thread; set aside. Weave a second strip with the same measurements.

*Strands:* Weave the working thread of one of the strips through the beads to exit from an edge bead on the strip's short side. Use G beads to make a single row of right angle weave 20 units long. Slip one of the beaded beads onto this row. Join this row to the corresponding edge bead on the other strip. Repeat, adding single rows between the strips with beaded beads attached, for a total of five strands connecting the strips. Secure the thread and trim (figure 10).

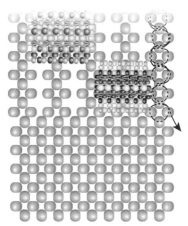

**figure 10**

## Clasp

Start a new double thread that exits from a G bead at the center of the seventh base row. Pick up three D beads, one H bead, nine C beads, and the ring side of the clasp; pass back through the H bead. Pick up three D beads and pass through the last G bead exited (figure 11). Repeat the thread path to reinforce. Secure the thread and trim.

**figure 11**

Repeat on the other side of the base to add the bar side of the clasp to the center of the fourth base row (figure 12).

**figure 12**

# Chapter 5

# NECKLACES

# GLIMMER NECKLACE

Sometimes less is more—and this design proves it. Layer a crystal disk pendant over a sparkling beadwoven circle, and hold them loosely together with a delicate right-angle-weave bail. A necklace of strung pearls and a beautiful stylized toggle clasp complete the design.

## SUPPLIES

Bronze size 15° seed beads, 2 g (A)

Bronze size 11° seed beads, 1 g (B)

Matte transparent light olivine size 11° seed beads, 1 g (C)

90 olivine crystal bicones, 3 mm (D)

46 dorado 2X crystal bicones, 3 mm (E)

55 olive crystal pearl round beads, 6 mm (F)

1 clear faceted crystal donut disk, 38 mm outside diameter, 15 mm inside diameter

2 gold decorative heishi beads, 2 x 3 mm

2 gold crimp tubes, 2 mm

1 gold decorative square toggle clasp, 22 mm

20 inches (50.8 cm) of beading wire

Thread

Wax

Needles

Scissors

Crimping pliers

## FINISHED SIZE

Pendant, 1¾ inches (4.5 cm) across

Necklace, 17½ inches (44.5 cm) long

## TECHNIQUES

Right angle weave

Diamond stitch

## Back Disk

*Round 1:* Use a single length of thread and A beads to make a strip of right angle weave 29 units long. Join the ends for a total of 30 units that form a ring. Exit from a top A bead (figure 1).

figure 1

*Round 2:* Work a round of circular right angle weave using A beads.

*Round 3:* Work a round of circular right angle weave using B beads.

*Round 4:* Pull the short end of the thread so that you're working with double thread. Work a round of circular right angle weave using D beads.

*Round 5:* Work a round of circular right angle weave using E beads for the sides and D beads for the top of each unit (figure 2). Secure the thread and trim. Set the disk aside.

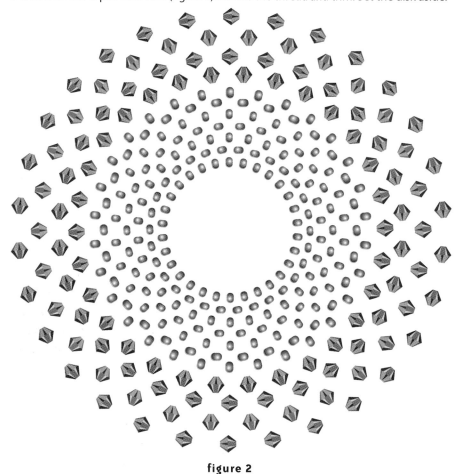

figure 2

## Bail

*Unit 1, round 1:* Pick up the following sequence four times: three C beads and one E bead. Tie the beads into a tight ring with an overhand knot, leaving a 3-inch (7.6 cm) tail. Pass through the first E bead (figure 3).

figure 3

*Unit 1, round 2:* Pick up one B bead and pass through the next E bead of round 1; repeat three times. Pass through the next two C beads (figure 4).

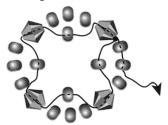

figure 4

*Connector:* Pick up one B bead, one C bead, and one B bead; pass through the last C bead exited and the next B and C beads.

*Unit 2, round 1:* Pick up one C bead and one E bead. String on the following three times: three C beads and one E bead. Pass through the last C exited in unit 1 and the next C and E beads.

*Unit 2, round 2:* Pick up one B bead and pass through the next E bead; repeat three times. Weave through the beads to exit from the C bead opposite the unit 1 and unit 2 connector.

## THE WAY IT MOVES
Suspended from a bail, the donut disk rotates freely in front of the fluid ring of beadwork. The glint of light off the crystal facets adds to the impression of movement.

*Strip:* Work three units of right angle weave with B beads and one unit of right angle weave with B beads on the top and bottom and one E bead on the side (figure 5). *Note:* This E bead will be the shared bead for the next diamond.

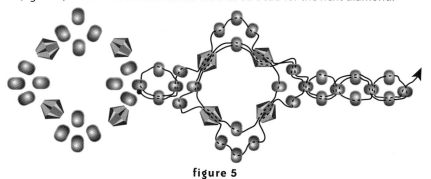

figure 5

Repeat two more diamond units and end with two units of right angle weave using B beads (figure 6).

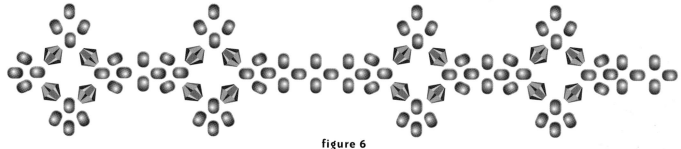

figure 6

## Necklace

**1** Use the beading wire to string one crimp tube, one heishi bead, 10 A beads, and one side of the clasp. Pass back through the heishi bead and the crimp tube. Use the crimping pliers to crimp the tube. String on this sequence 55 times: one F bead and one B bead. String one crimp tube, 1 heishi bead, and 10 A beads and the second half of the clasp. Pass back through the heishi bead and the crimp tube. Crimp the tube.

**2** Pass the bail through the center of the crystal donut disk and the beadwoven pendant. Fold the bail in half and join the last right-angle-weave unit to the beginning of the first diamond unit. Position the bail so the three right-angle-weave units are at the inside edge of the two pieces.

**3** Pass the toggle end of the necklace through the bail (figure 7).

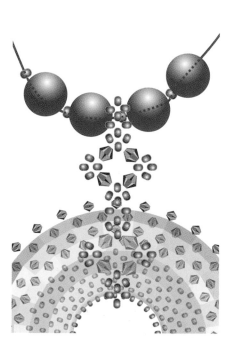

figure 7

**4** Weave through the bail beads to exit from the corner of the diamond unit sitting at the back of the beadwork. Stitch the side corners of the diamond to adjacent beads on the beadwoven pendant (figure 8).

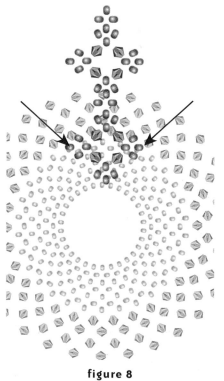

figure 8

Bronze size 15° seed beads, 2 g (A)

Bronze-lined clear size 11° seed beads, 6 g (B)

Aqua size 11° seed beads, 2 g (C)

Aqua matte size 8° seed beads, 4 g (D)

37 platinum crystal pearl round beads, 3 mm (E)

52 jet 2XAB crystal bicones, 3 mm (F)

2 clear crystal rivolis, 8 mm

Thread

Wax

Needles

Scissors

## FINISHED SIZE

Pendant, 1¾ inches (4.4 cm) across

Necklace, 19½ inches (49.3 cm) long

## TECHNIQUES

Peyote stitch

Ladder stitch

Right angle weave

# RIVETED NECKLACE

This sandwich of spokes is held together by a beaded rivet. A crystallized chain is given dimension by embellishments that appear on either side of it. A rivet and spoke component is used as the clasp, carrying the design full circle.

## Back Medallion

**1** Using double thread, pick up a stop bead, leaving a 12-inch (30.5 cm) tail. Pick up four D beads and three B beads. Pick up the following nine times: eight D beads and three B beads. Next, pick up four D beads, for a total of ten groups of three B beads. Don't push the beads all the way to the stop bead—leave some room on the thread. Pass back through the 11th, 10th, ninth, eighth, and seventh beads from the end of the initial strand (figure 1). Pull tightly to align the beads in two four-D-bead columns with a three-B-bead picot at the top, forming the first spoke.

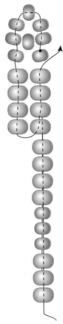

**figure 1**

**2** Pick up five B beads, skip the middle B bead of the picot, and pass down through the next B bead, through the four D beads beneath it, and up through the four D beads of the adjacent column (figure 2).

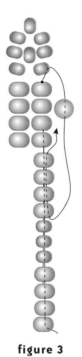

**figure 2**

**3** Pick up one E bead and pass through the next four D beads on the strand (figure 3). Pull tightly to align.

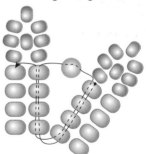

**figure 3**

**4** Pass through the next four D beads and the first B bead of the strand (figure 4).

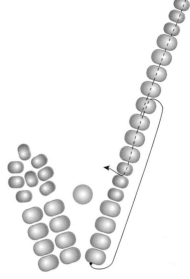

**figure 4**

**5** Repeat steps 2, 3, and 4 until all of the beads on the strand have been used.

**6** Close the beadwork into a ring by passing through the four D beads in the last column and the four D beads in the first column. Pick up one E bead and pass through the last column and the first column again (figure 5).

**figure 5**

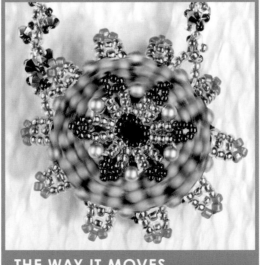

### THE WAY IT MOVES

The central layer in the pendant—a starburst of gold, aqua, and white seed beads and pearls—turns around a beaded "rivet" that's studded with a sparkling crystal rivoli.

**7** Repeat the thread path of the D-bead columns to reinforce (figure 6).

**figure 6**

## Spoke Tips

Weave through beads to exit from the third B bead at the point of one of the spokes. Pick up three C beads, skip the middle B bead, and pass down through the next three B beads, through the next E bead, and up through the next three B beads of the next spoke (figure 7). Repeat to add tips to all of the spokes. Weave through the beads to exit from a column of D beads toward the center. Leave on the working thread to complete the join later.

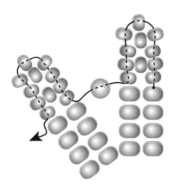

**figure 7**

## Front Medallion

Make a second medallion, this time using D, B, and E beads, only forming five spokes, and omitting the spoke tips. Start this medallion as with the back medallion, but to string the initial strand, pick up three D beads and three B beads, and pick up

this sequence four times: six D beads and three B beads. Finally, pick up three D beads. Finish the medallion as with the back medallion, but don't add the tips (figure 8).

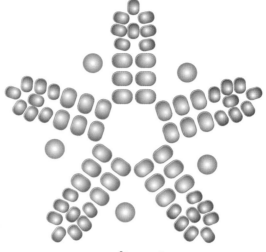

**figure 8**

## Join the Medallions

Position the front and back medallions with the insides of the spokes next to one another. Use the working thread left on the front medallion to pick up one B bead; pass through the opposite column of four D beads on the back medallion. Pass through the adjacent column of four D beads. Pick up one B bead; pass through the corresponding column of three D beads on the front medallion, the adjacent column, the E bead, and the column of D beads. Pick up one B bead, skip the next two columns of D beads on the back medallion, and enter the D beads of the next column. Pass through the D beads in the adjacent column. Pick up one B bead and pass through the column of D beads adjacent to the one you exited in the front medallion. Repeat around, skipping every other set of columns on the back medallion (figure 9).

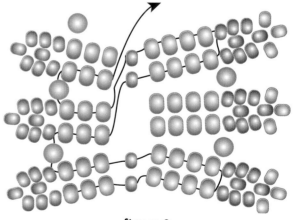

**figure 9**

## Front of the Rivet

**Base:** Use double thread and A beads to complete a strip of right angle weave 11 units long and two rows high. Join the short ends to form a base ring (figure 10).

**figure 10**

**Bezel:** Pass through each A bead on the edge of the ring and pull tightly to cup the beadwork. Place the rivoli face up in the cupped beadwork and weave through beads to exit from an A bead on the other edge of the ring. Pass through each A bead on the edge and pull tightly. Tie a half-hitch knot around threads to secure the thread tension (figure 11). Weave through beads to exit from the back edge of the bezel.

**figure 11**

**Round 1:** Pick up three A beads, skip the next A bead on the bezel's edge, and pass through the next A bead; repeat five times as you work your way around (figure 12). Pass through the first A bead added in this round.

**figure 12**

**Round 2:** Pick up one A bead and pass through the next A bead of the previous round; repeat to make your way completely around. Step up through the first A bead added in this round (figure 13).

**figure 13**

**Rounds 3–6:** Repeat round 2 four times, for a total of six rounds. Secure the thread and trim it. This is the rivet front for the pendant. Set aside.

Repeat this step *to round 3 only* to form the rivet front for the closure; set it aside.

## Backing for the Rivet

Follow the instructions for the back medallion, but for the initial strand, pick up three B beads and three A beads, and then string on this sequence five times: six B beads and three A beads. Finally, string on three B beads. Also make the following modifications:

- Use B, A, and E beads
- Form only six spokes
- Omit the spoke tips

Weave through beads to exit from a column of B beads toward the center. This is the rivet back for the pendant. Set it aside and repeat this step to form a backing for the closure. Set it aside, too.

## Join the Rivet

Pass the rivet front of the pendant through the front and back of the joined medallions. Position the last round of peyote stitch of the rivet front so it touches the interior of the rivet back for the pendant. Pass through the A bead on the edge of the peyote stitch, the next column of B beads on the spoke, the nearest E bead, and the next column of B beads. Repeat until each column of the rivet back is joined to the peyote-stitched round of the rivet front (figure 14). Set the pendant aside.

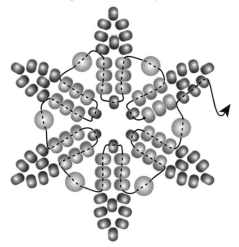

**figure 14**

Repeat this step to join the rivet front and backing for the closure. Set this item aside.

## Spinner Medallion

Follow the instructions for the back medallion, but begin by picking up three B beads and three A beads and then the following sequence nine times: six B beads and three A beads. Finally, pick up three B beads. Also make the following changes:

• Use B, A, and E beads
• Form 10 spokes
• Omit the spoke tips

Before adding the last E bead to form a ring, position the beadwork beneath the front medallion on the main pendant (figure 15). Secure the thread and trim.

**figure 15**

## Necklace Straps

Use double thread and B beads to make a strip of right angle weave 62 units long. Weave through beads to exit from the second shared bead from the end. Pick up three B beads and pass through the last B bead exited to form a picot, then continue through the next edge B bead and the following shared B bead, this time exiting from the other side of the strip (figure 16). Turn the strip over and repeat the picot sequence (figure 17).

**figure 16**

Continue adding picots, alternating between the front and back of the strip, for a total of 37 picots. Pick up one A bead, one F bead, and one A bead; pass through the next shared B bead from the opposite side so that the crystal lies diagonally across the right-angle-weave unit (figure 18). Turn the strip over and repeat. Repeat 25 times, alternating between the front and the back of the strip. Don't trim the thread. Set the strap aside.

**figure 17**

Repeat to form a second necklace strap.

**figure 18**

74

## Clasp

Attach a new thread at the beginning of one of the necklace straps. Pick up one B bead. Pass through the middle bead of one of the B-bead columns on the closure and the adjacent B bead in the opposite direction. Pick up one B bead and pass through the original B bead exited to form a right-angle-weave unit (figure 19). Repeat the thread path to reinforce.

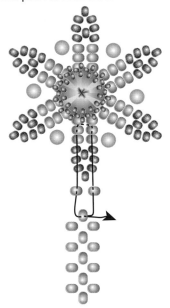

figure 19

Attach a new thread at the beginning of the other necklace strap. Pick up 29 A beads and pass back through the last B bead exited. Use B beads to work one round of circular peyote stitch (figure 20).

figure 20

## Attach the Necklace to the Pendant

Use the working thread left at the end of one of the necklace straps to pick up two B beads; pass through an E bead on the back medallion of the pendant. Pick up two B beads and pass through the last B bead exited (figure 21). Repeat the thread path to reinforce; secure the thread and trim.

figure 21

Join the other necklace strap to the third E bead from the first attachment.

Bronze gold size 15° seed beads, 1 g (A)

Matte purple size 15° seed beads, 5 g (B)

Matte cream size 15° seed beads, 1 g (C)

12 metallic pink/gold size 15° seed beads, 1 g (D)

Bronze size 11° seed beads, 1 g (E)

12 metallic pink/gold size 11° seed beads, 10 g (F)

Matte purple size 11° seed beads, 1 g (G)

Matte gold size 11° cylinder beads, 1 g (H)

31 gold aurum crystal round beads, 2 mm (I)

2 clear AB crystal round beads, 4 mm

1 purple haze crystal rondelle, 18 mm

1 bronze crystal lochrose bead, 4 mm

1 olive/cream shell donut disk, 35 mm outer diameter, 15 mm inner diameter

1 antique brass decorative toggle clasp, 12 mm

Thread

Wax

Needles

Scissors

**FINISHED SIZE**

Pendant, 3 inches (7.6 cm) long

Necklace, 26¾ inches (67.9 cm) long

**TECHNIQUE**

Right angle weave

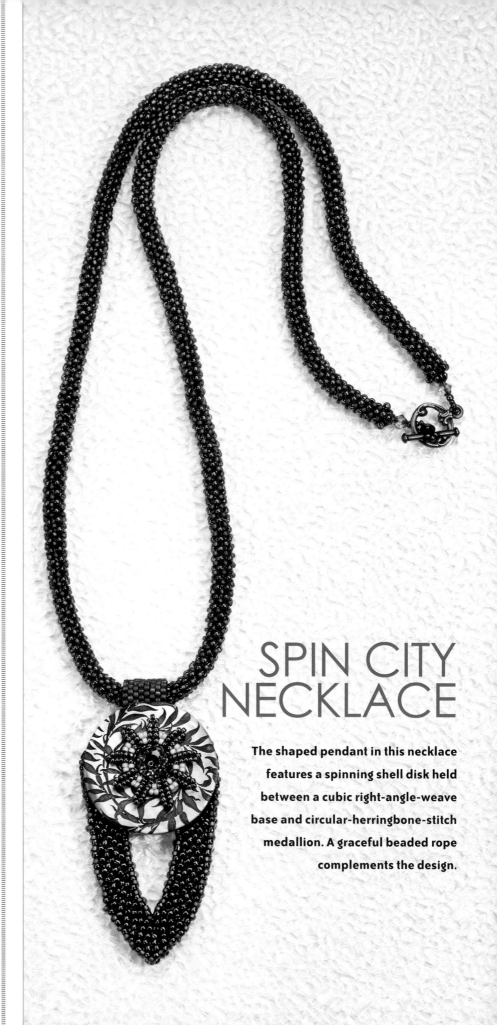

# SPIN CITY NECKLACE

The shaped pendant in this necklace features a spinning shell disk held between a cubic right-angle-weave base and circular-herringbone-stitch medallion. A graceful beaded rope complements the design.

## Pendant Base

Use single thread and E beads to make a strip of right angle weave that's 13 units wide and three rows high.

## Pendant Walls

**1** Weave through beads to exit from the third side bead in the third row, exiting away from the work. *Note:* This row will be woven at right angles to the base just completed.

Pick up three E beads; pass through the last E bead exited, the three E beads just added, and the next E bead in the same row of the base to form the first unit. Pick up two E beads; pass down through the side E bead of the previous unit, the last E bead exited on the base, and the first E bead just added to form the second unit. Pick up two E beads; pass through the next base bead, the side E bead of the previous unit, and the two E beads just added to form the third unit (figure 1).

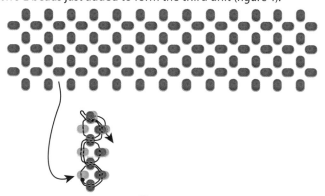

**figure 1**

### THE WAY IT MOVES
The shell disk held between the cubic right-angle-weave base and circular-herringbone-stitch medallion is held on by a decorative rivet that allows it to spin.

**2** Pass through a top E bead on the next base row and the nearest side bead on the base.

You've completed one wall of right angle weave at right angles to the base. Repeat this entire step along the base until you have 10 walls. *Note:* The first and last walls will be formed by folding up the base (figure 2).

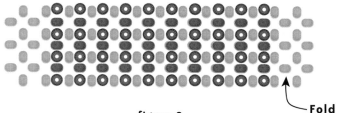

**figure 2**

— Fold

## Join the Wall Tops and Sides

**3** Weave through beads to exit from the first side bead on the short edge of the base. Pick up one E bead and pass through the mirror top bead of the first wall. Pick up one E bead; pass through the last base E bead exited, the first E bead just added, the mirror wall bead, the second E bead just added, and the next top wall bead (this will be an edge bead). This is the first top unit.

**4** Pick up one E bead and pass through the mirror bead of the first wall, the second E bead added in the previous unit, the first edge bead exited, and the bead just added.

**5** Repeat to connect the third edge bead to the first wall. Start the next row by connecting the first top bead of the first wall to the mirror bead of the second wall (figure 3).

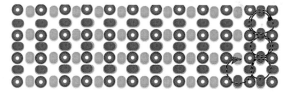

**figure 3**

Repeat until all walls are joined by top beads, connecting the 10th wall to the edge beads at the end of the base.

## Pointed Curve

**6** Weave through beads to exit from a top edge bead on the bottom right corner of the cubic right-angle-weave base. Use E beads and right angle weave to make a strip three units across and 20 rows long (figure 4).

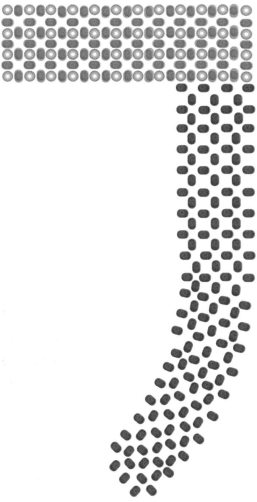

**figure 4**

**7** Weave through beads to exit from the inside edge bead of the 20th row just stitched. Still in right angle weave, make three units (figure 5). *Note: This is row 4 of the second side of the pointed curve.*

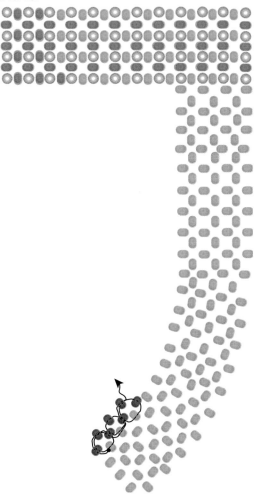

**figure 5**

**8** Continuing in right angle weave, stitch three units across and 15 rows long. Join the end row to the top edge on the bottom left corner of the base to form a 20th row (figure 6).

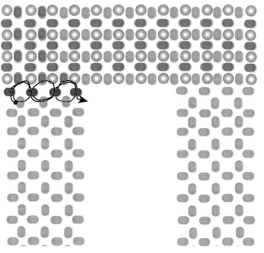

**figure 6**

**9** Repeat steps 6 and 7 to stitch a matching pointed curve in right angle weave, this time working off of the bottom beads of the base.

## Join the Inside and Outside Edges

Weave through beads to exit from the first inside edge bead of the bottom pointed curve, near the bottom of the cubic right-angle-weave base. Use G beads to connect the top and bottom pointed curves, forming an inside edge (figure 7).

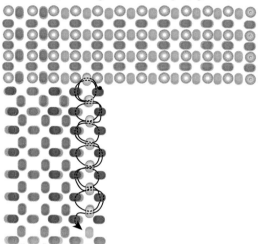

**figure 7**

Repeat on the outside edge using I beads (figure 8).

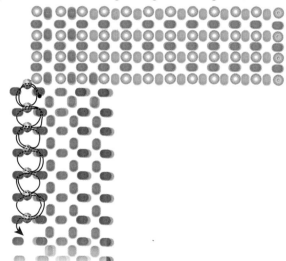

**figure 8**

## Embellish the Edges

Weave through beads to exit from the top E bead at the top left corner of the base. Pick up one B bead and pass through the next E bead; repeat to embellish the top outside edge of the pendant. Weave through beads to exit from a top inside edge E bead. Pick up one B bead and pass through the next E bead; repeat to embellish the top inside edge of the pendant (figure 9).

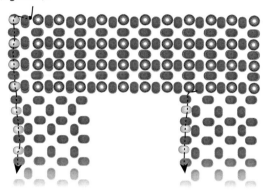

**figure 9**

## Bail

Weave through beads to exit from the fourth E bead along the top edge at the front of the base. Pick up one H bead and pass through the next E bead; repeat three times for a total of four H beads. Use H beads to work a strip of peyote stitch 44 rows long. Fold the strip so the final row touches the bottom edge of the back of the base. Zip the final row of H beads to the E beads, forming a bail (figure 10).

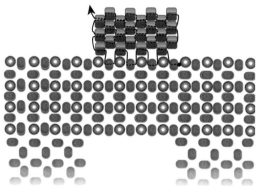

**figure 10**

## Necklace

Use double thread to make a five-unit tubular right-angle-weave rope with B beads for the sides and F beads for the top and bottom of each unit. It should measure 25 inches (63.5 cm), or the desired length minus the clasp width (figure 11).

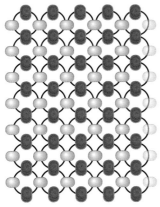

**figure 11**

## Attach the Clasp

Start a new length of double thread that exits ½ inch (1.3 cm) from the end of the rope. Weave through beads to exit inside the tube and out through the end. String one 4-mm bicone, one E bead, six D beads, and one half of the clasp; pass back through the E bead and bicone and back into the rope. Exit from a bead on the rope, then secure the thread and trim. Repeat to add the second half of the clasp to the other end of the rope (figure 12).

**figure 12**

## Spinner

*Base ring:* You'll use single thread and A beads to make a ladder-stitched strip three beads high and 18 columns wide. Start by picking up a stop bead and passing back through it. Pick up 54 A beads; *skip the last three beads strung and pass through the next three beads in the direction they were strung. Pull gently to align the columns (figure 13). Repeat from * to form a total of 18 columns.

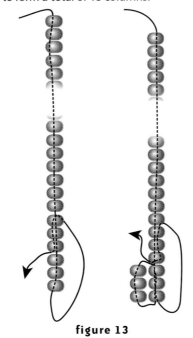

**figure 13**

Exiting up through the final column, pass down through the first column and back up through the final column to form a ring (figure 14).

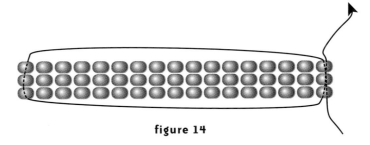

**figure 14**

*Round 1 :* Pick up two A beads, then pass down through the next A bead of the base ring and up through the next A bead; repeat eight times for a total of nine groups of two beads.

*Round 2:* Pick up two A beads; pass down through the next A bead of the previous round. Pick up one C bead; pass up through the next A bead of the previous round. Repeat around, then step up through the first A bead added in this round.

*Round 3:* Pick up two A beads; pass down through the next A bead of the previous round. Pick up two C beads; pass up through the next A bead of the previous round. Repeat around, then step up through the first A bead added in this round.

*Round 4:* Pick up two A beads; pass down through the next A bead of the previous round, through the next two C beads of the previous round, and up through the top A bead of the next column. Repeat around, then step up through the top two A beads of the first column.

*Round 5:* Pick up three A beads; pass down through the next A bead of the previous round and the two A beads below it, through the next two C beads of round 3, and up through the top two A beads of the next column. Repeat around. Weave through beads to exit from the other side of the original ladder (figure 15).

**figure 15**

Pass the ladder-stitched ring through the hole in the shell disk.

## Spinner Back

*Round 1:* Turn the spinner over. Pick up one A bead; pass down through the next ladder bead and up through the following ladder bead. Repeat around for a total of nine A beads. Step up through the first A bead added in this round.

*Round 2:* Pick up one C bead and pass through the next A bead; repeat around and step up through the first C bead added in this round.

*Round 3:* Pick up one A bead and pass through the next C bead; repeat around and step up through the first A bead added in this round.

*Round 4:* Pick up two A beads and pass through the next A bead; repeat around and step up through the first two A beads added in this round.

*Round 5:* Pick up one H bead and pass through the next two A beads; repeat around and step up through the first H bead added in this round.

*Round 6:* Pick up three A beads and pass through the next H bead; repeat around and step up through the first three A beads added in this round.

*Round 7:* Pick up one H bead and pass through the next three A beads; repeat around and step up through the first H bead added in this round.

*Round 8:* Pick up three A beads and pass through the next H bead; repeat around and step up through the first three A beads added in this round.

*Round 9:* Pick up two H beads and pass through the next three A beads; repeat around and step up through the first two H beads added in this round (figure 16).

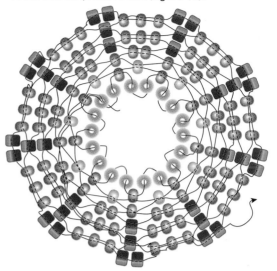

**figure 16**

## Attach the Spinner

Position the spinner so the back touches the front center of the top of the pendant. Securely stitch round 9 of the spinner back to the base beads.

Weave through beads to exit out through the center of the spinner. Pick up one rondelle, one lochrose bead, and one A bead; pass back through the lochrose bead, the rondelle, and the spinner, and sew into the base (figure 17). Repeat the thread path to reinforce. Secure the threads and trim.

**figure 17**

## SUPPLIES

Light gray size 15° seed beads, 1 g (A)

Dark gray size 15° seed beads, 1 g (B)

Silver size 11° cylinder beads, 2 g (C)

Beige-lined clear size 11° seed beads, 8 g (D)

Gray size 11° seed beads, 2 g (E)

176 platinum crystal pearl round beads, 3 mm (F)

32 platinum crystal pearl round beads, 4 mm (G)

176 light metallic gold crystal round beads, 2 mm (H)

2 dark gray crystal rondelles, 7 x 12 mm

1 smoky topaz crystal rondelle, 7 x 12 mm

3 sand opal crystal lochrose beads, 4 x 2 mm

Thread

Wax

Needles

Scissors

## FINISHED SIZE

Pendant, 1⅜ x 3 inches (3.5 x 7.6 cm)

Necklace, 18 inches (45.7 cm) long

## TECHNIQUES

Peyote stitch

Right angle weave

Spiral rope

Ladder stitch

Brick stitch

# GABRIELLA NECKLACE

Crystal rondelles play peek-a-boo, cupped in the center of two sculptural medallions that appear to float from a crystal- and pearl-studded spiral rope.

## Large Medallion

*Round 1:* Thread 72 inches (1.8 m) of thread and double it. Pull one end of the thread so you have a 12-inch (30.5 cm) length of single thread. Pick up four A beads and position them 4 inches (10.2 cm) from the end of the doubled thread; tie a double overhand knot. *Note:* The single tail thread will be used to complete rounds of peyote stitch later in the process.

Complete 17 units of right angle weave and join the last unit to the first so you have a ring with a total of 18 units. Exit from a top A bead.

*Round 2:* Work a round of tubular right angle weave using one A bead for each side and one D bead for the top of each unit. Exit from a top D bead.

*Round 3:* Still in tubular right angle weave, work a round using D beads. Exit from a top D bead.

*Round 4:* Continue in tubular right angle weave, using one F bead and one D bead for each side and one G bead for the top of each unit (figure 1).

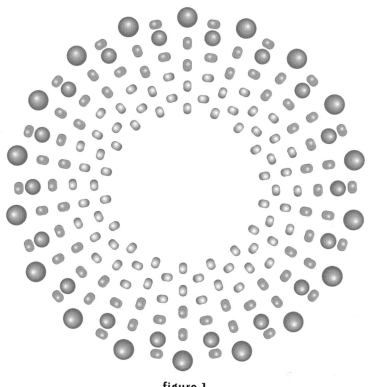

**figure 1**

*Round 5:* Weave through beads to exit from a D bead at the top of round 3. Pick up one D bead and pass through the next D bead; repeat around. Pass through the first D bead added.

*Round 6:* Pick up one H bead and pass through the next D bead added in this step; repeat around. Secure the thread and trim (figure 2).

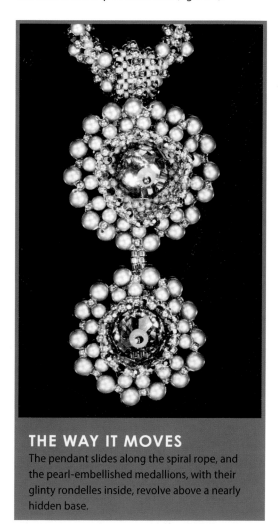

### THE WAY IT MOVES
The pendant slides along the spiral rope, and the pearl-embellished medallions, with their glinty rondelles inside, revolve above a nearly hidden base.

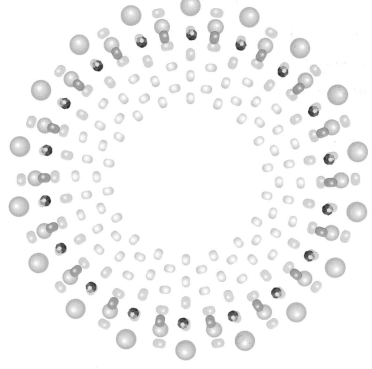

**figure 2**

*Round 7 (back):* Weave the medallion's tail thread through beads to exit from a bottom A bead of round 1. Pick up one A bead and pass through the next two A beads of round 1; repeat around and step up through the first bead added in this round.

*Round 8 (back):* Pick up one A bead and pass through the next A bead; repeat around for a total of nine beads. Step up through the first bead added in this round.

*Round 9 (back):* Pick up one A bead and pass through the next two A beads of round 8; repeat three times. Step up through the first bead added in this round.

*Round 10 (back):* Pick up one A bead and pass through the next two A beads; repeat for a total of four beads. Pick up one A bead and go through the next A bead. Pull gently to tighten. Secure the thread and trim (figure 3). Set the beadwork aside.

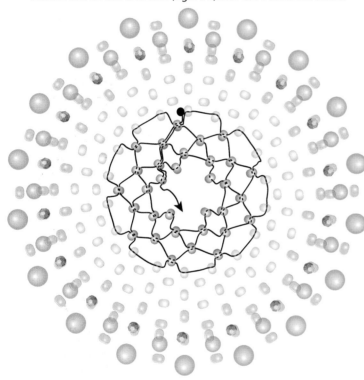

figure 3

## Small Medallion

Follow along with figure 4.

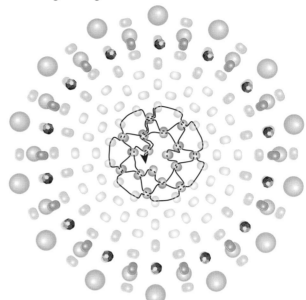

figure 4

*Rounds 1–6:* Repeat rounds 1–6 of the large medallion, this time starting with 13 units and joining the ends so the ring has a total of 14 units.

*Round 7 (back):* Weave the tail thread through beads to exit from a bottom A bead of round 1. Pick up one A bead and pass through the next two A beads of round 1; repeat around and step up through the first bead added in this round.

*Round 8 (back):* Pick up one A bead and pass through the next A bead of round 7; repeat around for a total of seven beads. Step up through the first bead added in this round.

*Round 9 (back):* Pick up one A bead and pass through the next two A beads twice. Pick up one A bead and pass through the next three A beads. Pull gently to tighten. Secure the thread and trim.

## Base

**1** Use double thread and C beads to ladder stitch a strip 12 beads across.

**2** Decreasing one bead in each row, use C beads to work eight rows of brick stitch until four beads remain. Weave through beads to exit out from the first bead of the original ladder-stitched strip. Decreasing one bead in each row, use C beads to work 10 rows of brick stitch until two beads remain. Work seven rows of square stitch off of these two beads.

**3** Work brick stitch for eight rows, increasing one bead in each row for a total of 10 beads in the final row. Complete eight additional rows, decreasing one bead in each row, until two beads remain (figure 5).

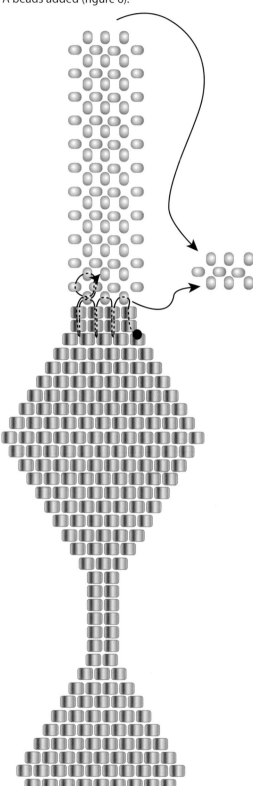

**figure 5**

## Bail

**4** Attach a new single thread that exits from an edge C bead at the top of the larger diamond. Work one row of square stitch four C beads across. Exit up through an end C bead. String one A bead, pass down through the next C bead and the one beneath it, turn, and pass up through the next two C beads to return to the top; repeat to add a total of three A beads. Exit from the final A bead added.

**5** Use A beads to make a strip of right angle weave that's three units wide and 12 rows long off of the last three A beads added (figure 6).

**figure 6**

**6** Fold the strip in half and join the edge beads of the 12th row to the three A beads added at the top of the square stitch.

### Embellish the Bail

Weave through beads to exit from an edge A bead of the bail. Pick up one B bead and pass through the next edge A bead; repeat for a total of 12 beads. Repeat this embellishment on the next three vertical rows. Weave through beads to exit from a B bead on the second row nearest the joining row. Pick up one D bead and pass through the opposite B bead on the third row. Pick up one D bead and pass through the first B bead, the last D bead added, and the next B bead. Continue adding D beads until all of the center B beads have been joined (figure 7).

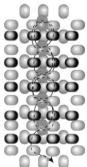

**figure 7**

## Connect the Medallions

**7** Start a new double thread that exits from the sixth bead of the middle row of the top diamond. Pass through the hole at the center of the large medallion. Pick up one dark gray crystal rondelle, one lochrose bead, and one B bead. Pass back through the lochrose bead, the rondelle, and the center of the medallion. Pass through the seventh bead of the diamond's middle row. Repeat the thread path to reinforce.

**8** Weave through beads to exit from the middle of the smaller diamond and repeat step 7, using the fifth and sixth beads of the middle row of the diamond and the small medallion (figure 8). You've now finished the pendant; set it aside.

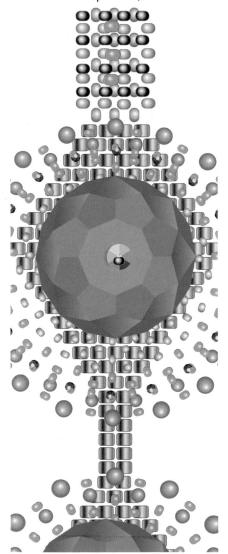

**figure 8**

## Spiral Rope

**9** Use a double length of thread to pick up one D bead, one H bead, one D bead, and four E beads. Pass back through the D, H, and D beads (figure 9).

**figure 9**

**10** Pull the thread tight to align the beads into two columns. *Note:* The E beads create the core of the spiral and the D, H, and D beads are the first set of outside beads (figure 10).

**figure 10**

**11** Pick up one E bead, one D bead, one F bead, and one D bead. Pass up through the top three E beads from step 9 and the E bead just added. Pull the thread gently to align the beads and use your fingers to push the new set of beads next to the first set. *Note:* One core bead and the second set of outside beads were added (figure 11).

**figure 11**

**12** Continue adding one new core bead and alternating between set one (D, H, and D beads) and set two (D, F, and D beads) for the outside beads (figure 12) until the rope measures 18 inches (45.7 cm).

**figure 12**

## Closure

On one end of the spiral rope, pick up one F bead and 25 D beads. Pass through the first D bead just added. Work three rounds of circular peyote stitch with D beads. *Note:* Rounds one and two are formed by the 25-bead loop. Repeat the thread path to reinforce. Pass back though the first F bead added in this section, secure the thread, and trim (figure 13).

**figure 13**

On the other end of the spiral rope, pick up one F bead, the smoky topaz rondelle, one lochrose bead, and one B bead. Pass back through the lochrose bead, the rondelle, and the F bead (figure 14). Repeat the thread path to reinforce. Secure the thread and trim.

**figure 14**

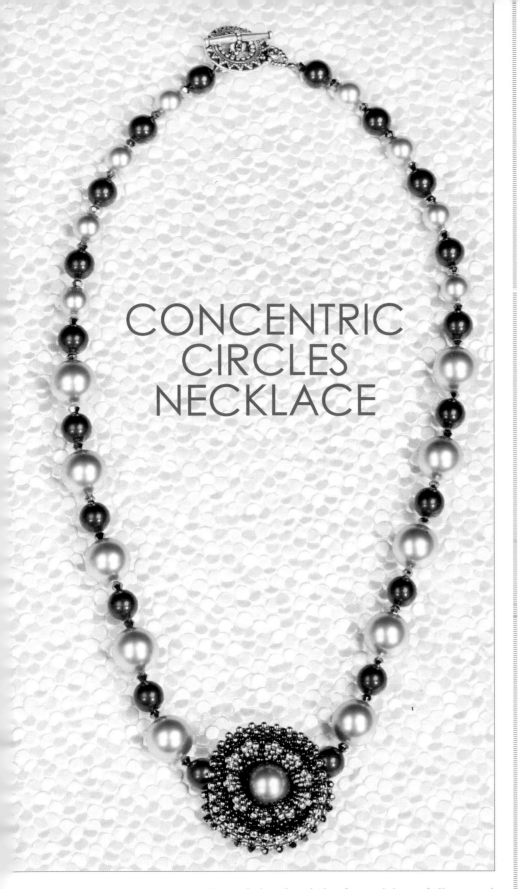

# CONCENTRIC CIRCLES NECKLACE

## SUPPLIES

Metallic silver size 15° seed beads, 1 g (A)

Metallic dark blue size 15° seed beads, 1 g (B)

Metallic silver blue size 11° seed beads, 1 g (C)

Metallic silver size 11° seed beads, 3 g (D)

30 light metallic gold crystal rounds, 2 mm

40 light metallic gold crystal bicones, 3 mm

20 dark blue crystal pearl rounds, 6 mm

8 light gray crystal pearl rounds, 6 mm

11 light gray crystal pearl rounds, 12 mm

2 silver crimp tubes, 2 mm

1 silver toggle clasp

Thread

Wax

2 feet (61 cm) of beading wire

Needles

Scissors

Crimping pliers

Wire cutters

## FINISHED SIZE

Focal element, 1¼ inches (3.2 cm) across

Necklace, 19½ inches (49.3 cm) long

## TECHNIQUES

Peyote stitch

Right angle weave

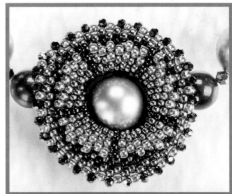

## THE WAY IT MOVES
The focal element spins on its axis to reveal a different colorway on the flip side.

With its multiple layers and supple beadwork that forms delicate frills around a central bead nestled within, the focal element of this piece looks much like a rosette or cockade—those ribbon ornaments worn on the hats of French revolutionaries. Speaking of revolutions, the focal element revolves on the beading wire upon which all the beads are strung.

## Large Ring, Inside

*Row 1:* Use B beads to make a strip of right angle weave 29 units long. Exit from a top B bead.

*Row 2:* Pick up three B beads and pass through the last B bead exited, then pick up one A bead and pass through the next top B bead in row 1; repeat 28 times for a total of 29 B-bead units with A beads between them (figure 1).

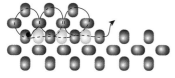

**figure 1**

Join the strip into a ring using B beads (figure 2). Exit from a top B bead in row 2. *Note:* Because the work has become tubular, the rows will now be referred to as rounds.

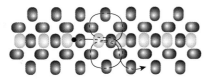

**figure 2**

## Large Ring, Side 1

*Round 3:* Pick up one B bead and pass through the next B bead in round 2; repeat 29 times for a total of 30 peyote-stitched B beads. Step up for the next and subsequent rounds by passing through the first bead added in the current round.

*Round 4:* Pick up one A bead and pass through the next B bead in round 3; repeat 29 times for a total of 30 A beads.

*Round 5:* Pick up one B bead and pass through the next A bead in round 4; repeat 29 times for a total of 30 B beads.

*Round 6:* Pick up one D bead and pass through the next B bead in round 5; repeat 29 times for a total of 30 D beads. Weave through beads to exit from the bottom B bead of round 1 (figure 3).

**figure 3**

## Large Ring, Side 2

*Round 7:* Pick up one B bead and pass through the next B bead in round 2; repeat 29 times for a total of 30 B beads.

*Round 8:* Pick up one A bead and pass through the next B bead in round 7; repeat 29 times for a total of 30 A beads.

*Round 9:* Pick up one B bead and pass through the next A bead in round 8; repeat 29 times for a total of 30 B beads.

*Round 10:* Pick up one D bead and pass through the next B bead in round 9; repeat 29 times for a total of 30 D beads.

*Round 11:* Pick up one D bead and pass through the next D bead in round 10; repeat 29 times for a total of 30 D beads.

*Round 12:* Pick up one D bead and pass through the next D bead in round 11; repeat 29 times for a total of 30 D beads.

*Round 13:* Pick up a 2-mm crystal bead and pass through the next D bead in round 12; repeat 29 times for a total of

thirty 2-mm crystal beads (figure 4). Weave in the thread and trim. Set this ring aside.

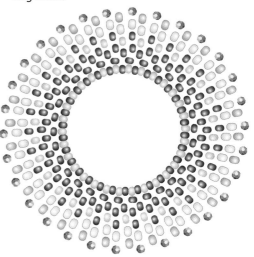

**figure 4**

## Small Ring, Center

*Row 1:* Use B beads to form a strip of right angle weave 19 units long. Exit from a top B bead.

*Row 2:* Pick up three B beads and pass through the last B bead exited, then pick up one A bead and pass through the next top B bead in row 1; repeat 18 times for a total of 19 units.

Use one B bead to join the strip into a ring. Exit from a top B bead in row 1. *Note:* As before, because the work has become tubular, the rows will now be referred to as rounds.

## Small Ring, Side 1

*Round 3:* Pick up one A bead and pass through the next B bead in round 1; repeat twice. Pick up one B bead and pass through the next B bead in round 2. Repeat the pattern of adding three A beads then one B bead four times, for a total of 15 A beads and five B beads. Step up for the next and subsequent rounds by passing through the first bead of the current round.

*Round 4:* Pick up one A bead and pass through the next bead in round 3; repeat 19 times for a total of 20 A beads.

*Round 5:* Repeat round 3, working off of round 4.

*Round 6:* Pick up one D bead and pass through the next bead in round 5; repeat 19 times for a total of 20 D beads.

*Round 7:* Repeat round 3, this time using C and D beads and working off of round 6.

*Round 8:* Pick up one D bead and pass through the next bead in round 7; repeat 19 times for a total of 20 D beads. Weave through beads to exit from a D bead in this round that sits before a D bead in round 7.

*Round 9:* Pick up one C bead and pass through the D beads in rounds 7 and 8 to exit from the next D bead in round 8 that sits before a C bead in round 7; repeat four times for a total of five C beads (figure 5). Weave through beads to exit from a bottom B bead of round 1.

**figure 5**

## Small Ring, Side 2

*Round 10:* Pick up a B bead and pass through the next B bead in round 1, then pick up one A bead and pass through the next B bead in round 1; repeat nine times for a total of 10 B beads and 10 A beads.

*Round 11:* Pick up one A bead and pass through the next bead in round 10; repeat 19 times for a total of 20 A beads.

*Round 12:* Repeat round 10, working off of round 11.

*Round 13:* Pick up one D bead and pass through the next bead in round 12; repeat 19 times for a total of 20 D beads.

*Round 14:* Repeat round 10, this time using C and D beads and working off of round 13 (figure 6). Weave in the thread and trim.

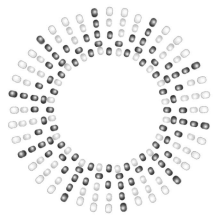

**figure 6**

Position the smaller ring inside the larger ring to create the focal element.

## Necklace

**1** String on one crimp bead, seven A beads, and one half of the clasp onto the beading wire. Pass back through the crimp bead, pull the wire snug, and crimp the bead with crimping pliers.

**2** String on one 3-mm crystal, one blue 6-mm pearl, one 3-mm crystal, and one gray 6-mm pearl. Repeat three times for a total of four groups.

**3** String on one 3-mm crystal, one blue 6-mm pearl, one 3-mm crystal, and one gray 12-mm pearl. Repeat four times for a total of five groups.

**4** String on one 3-mm crystal, one blue 6-mm pearl, and one 3-mm crystal.

**5** Pass the beading wire between the seed beads of round 1 of one side of the focal element. String on one A bead, one gray 12-mm pearl, and one A bead;

pass the beading wire between the seed beads of round 1 of the focal element on the opposite side.

**6** String beads on the second half of the beading wire to match the first half. Pick up one crimp bead, seven A beads, and the other half of the clasp. Pass back through the crimp bead, pull the beads snug, and crimp the bead. Use wire cutters to trim any excess wire (figure 7).

**figure 7**

## SUPPLIES

Silver size 11° seed beads, 34 g (A)

Matte black size 11° seed beads, 7 g (B)

Shiny black one-cut size 8° seed beads, 24 g (C)

15 silver shade rose montée beads, 6 mm (D)

Thread

Wax

Needles

Scissors

## FINISHED SIZE

Adjustable to 26 inches (66 cm)

## TECHNIQUES

Tubular herringbone

Tubular right angle weave

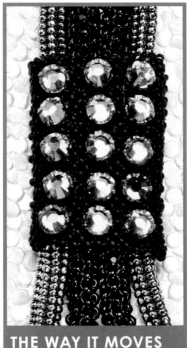

### THE WAY IT MOVES
When you run the slider up and down the ropes, it almost sounds like a zipper.

# CHRISTINA NECKLACE

Stitch two luscious ropes and capture them inside a flirty slide studded with crystals. For a glamorous look, move the slide to choker length; sliding it midway or low looks great for day wear.

## Herringbone Stitch Rope

Use double thread and A beads to stitch a herringbone tube three columns around and 30 inches (76.2 cm) long. Stitch the ends together to form a circle (figure 1). Secure the thread and trim. Set it aside.

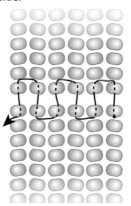

**figure 1**

## Right Angle Weave Rope

Use double thread and C beads to make a tube of right angle weave that's three units around and 28½ inches (72.4 cm) long. Measure to make sure that when joined, this tube will be short enough to lie inside the herringbone stitch rope. Join the ends (figure 2). Secure the thread and trim. Set it aside.

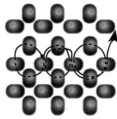

**figure 2**

## Slide

Use double thread and B beads to make a strip of right angle weave 23 units wide and 16 rows long. Don't trim the thread. *Note:* In the very last step, when the sides of this piece are joined to form a loop, it should encircle both ropes snugly. You may need more or less than 23 rows to ensure enough friction to keep the slide in place. Test it around the two ropes; adjust the width so the slide will fit tightly around them, but can still slide if you apply pressure.

## Embellish the Slide

Follow along with figure 3. Start a new double thread that exits from a B bead. Pick up one D bead through the diagonal back channel and pass through the

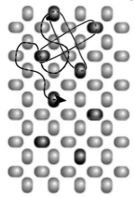

**figure 3**

opposite bead. Weave through the B beads to exit from the opposite corner B bead and pass through the second diagonal back channel of the D just added. Weave through the B beads to exit from the next group of B beads. Repeat to add five D beads per column across three columns (figure 4). Weave through the B beads to exit from a side B bead on the short edge of the strip.

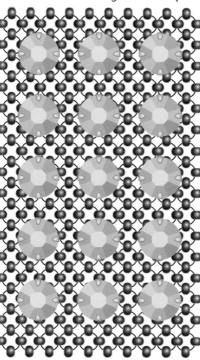

**figure 4**

## Attach the Slide

Wrap the strip around both ropes. Use B beads and the working thread left untrimmed on the slide to join the sides of the embellished strip of right angle weave around the two ropes (figure 5).

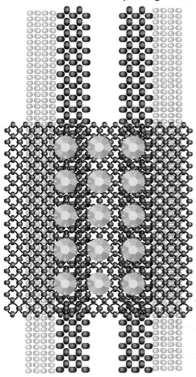

**figure 5**

Silver size 15° seed beads, 1 g (A)

Blue size 11° seed beads, 4 g (B)

20 dark gray crystal pearl round beads, 3 mm (C)

38 sapphire crystal round beads, 2 mm (D)

2 black diamond lochrose beads, 4 x 2 mm

2 Montana crystal bicones, 6 mm

2 black diamond AB crystal bicones, 8 mm

2 silver shade crystal heart-shaped pendants, 12 x 10 mm

2 black diamond crystal-encrusted beads, 10 mm

2 Montana crystal-encrusted beads, 10 mm

1 silver shade crystal-encrusted oval bead, 15 x 12 mm

2 gunmetal jump rings, 6 mm, 22 gauge

3 gunmetal head pins, 22 gauge

15 inches (38.1 cm) of gunmetal wire, 22 gauge

10 inches (25.4 cm) of gunmetal fine chain, 1.5 mm wide

56 inches (1.4 m) of gunmetal long-and-short textured chain, 8 x 6 mm by 3 x 4 mm

Thread

Wax

Needles

Scissors

Wire cutters

Round-nose pliers

Chain-nose pliers

## FINISHED SIZE

Tassel, 3½ inches (8.9 cm) long

Necklace, 30 inches (76.2 cm) long

## TECHNIQUE

Cubic right angle weave

# TASSEL NECKLACE

Adding tiny crystals along the front edges of a small band of cubic right angle weave causes it to curve. Add a row of small pearls, then suspend a variety of crystal dangles from the band using fine chain. The result is a swinging, thoroughly modern tassel.

## Base

Use single thread and B beads to make a strip of cubic right angle weave three units wide and 13 units long (figure 1).

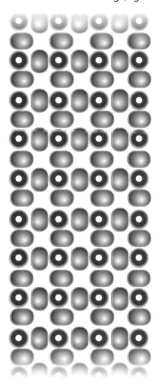

figure 1

## Base Ends

**1** Weave through beads to exit from a side wall B bead on one end of the base.

Work cubic right angle weave to form three cubes along the short end of the strip, using B beads on the sides and C beads on the top (figure 2).

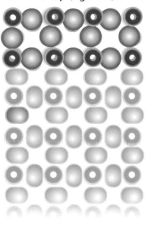

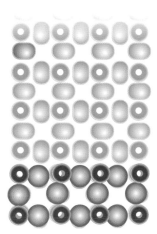

figure 2

**2** Weave through beads to exit from a top C bead. Pick up one D bead and pass through the next C bead; repeat around the edge of these three new cubes for a total of eight D beads (figure 3).

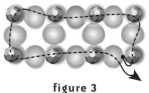

figure 3

**3** Repeat steps 1 and 2 on the opposite end of the base, taking care that this new set of cubes faces the same way as the first set. *Note:* These base ends will sit underneath the base when the necklace is worn. Weave through beads to exit from the end B bead on the top long edge on the front of the base, toward the work.

## Curve the Base

**4** "Pass through the next B bead on the top front long edge and pull tight to begin to curve the base. Repeat, passing through each B bead on this edge without adding a bead.

**THE WAY IT MOVES**
A flashy fringe of chain and beads does the salsa, catching everyone's attention.

**5** Weave through beads to exit from the second B bead on the bottom long edge on the front of the base. Pick up one D bead and pass through the next B bead; repeat along the entire bottom long edge at the front of the base (figure 4).

figure 4

**6** Weave through the beads to exit from the top edge at the back of the base. Repeat from * (in step 4), adding no beads between B beads along the top edge and one D bead between each B bead along the bottom edge at the back of the base.

**7** Weave through beads to exit from the bottom B bead of the seventh base cube on the bottom of the base (figure 5). Set aside.

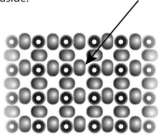

figure 5

## Cut the Chain

Cut the fine chain to the following lengths, then set them aside.

- 3 pieces ½ inch (1.3 cm) long
- 3 pieces 1 inch (2.5 cm) long
- 1 piece ¾ inch (1.9 cm) long
- 1 piece 1¼ inches (3.2 cm) long
- 1 piece ¼ inch (6 mm) long
- 1 piece 1⅛ inches (2.9 cm) long

As you make the drops in the next five steps, follow along with figure 6.

Drop 5

Drop 4

Drop 3

Drop 2

Center drop

figure 6

## Center Drop

Slide one lochrose bead, one oval crystal-encrusted bead, and one lochrose bead onto a head pin. Form a wrapped loop that connects to the end of a ½-inch (1.3 cm) piece of chain. Cut 3 inches (7.6 cm) of wire and form a wrapped loop that connects to the other end of the chain just attached. Use this wire to string one 8-mm bicone, then form a wrapped loop that connects to a 1¼-inch (3.2 cm) piece of chain.

Pass the working thread on the base through the top link of chain in the drop just formed. Pass through the last B bead exited to secure the drop. Repeat the thread path several times to reinforce. Weave through beads to exit from the bottom B bead of the fifth base cube.

## Drop 2

Use one jump ring to connect one heart-shaped pendant and a ½-inch (1.3 cm) piece of chain. Cut 3 inches (7.6 cm) of wire and form a wrapped loop that connects to the other end of the chain just attached. Use this wire to string one Montana 10-mm crystal-encrusted bead, then form a wrapped loop that connects to a 1-inch (2.5 cm) piece of chain. Sew this drop to the base where the thread exits, as with the previous drop. Weave through beads to exit from the bottom B bead of the third base cube.

## Drop 3

Slide one 8-mm bicone onto a head pin. Form a wrapped loop that connects to the end of a 1-inch (2.5 cm) piece of chain. Cut 3 inches (7.6 cm) of wire and form a wrapped loop that connects to the other end of the chain just attached. Use this wire to string one 6-mm bicone, then form a wrapped loop that connects to the end of a ¾-inch (1.9 cm) piece of chain. Attach to the base as before. Weave through beads to exit from the bottom B bead of the ninth base cube.

## Drop 4

Slide one Montana 10-mm crystal-encrusted bead onto a head pin. Form a wrapped loop that connects to the end of a 1⅛-inch (2.9 cm) piece of chain. Cut 3 inches (7.6 cm) of wire and form a wrapped loop to connect to the other end of the chain just attached. Use this wire to string one black diamond 10-mm crystal-encrusted bead, then form another wrapped loop that connects to the end of a ¼-inch (6 mm) piece of chain. Attach to the base. Weave through beads to exit from the bottom B bead of the 11th base cube.

## Drop 5

Use one jump ring to connect one heart-shaped pendant and the end of a ½-inch (1.3 cm) piece of chain. Cut 3 inches (7.6 cm) of wire, then form a wrapped loop that connects to the other end of the chain just placed. Use this wire to string one 6-mm bicone, then form a wrapped loop that connects to the end of a 1-inch (2.5 cm) piece of chain. Attach to the base. Secure the thread and trim.

## Attach the Neck Chain

Cut two pieces of long-and-short chain, each 28 inches (71.1 cm) long; set aside.

Attach a new double thread that exits from the second D bead on the top edge at one end of the base. Pick up the following four times: two A beads and one B bead, for a total of 12 beads strung. Then pick up two A beads and the links at one end of each chain. Pass through the third D bead on the same end of the base to form a loop. Repeat the thread path to reinforce; secure the thread and trim. Repeat this step on the top edge at the other end of the base (figure 7).

**figure 7**

## SUPPLIES

**Bronze size 15° seed beads, 2 g (A)**

**Aqua size 15° seed beads, 2 g (B)**

**Pink/gold size 15° seed beads, 2 g (C)**

**Bronze size 11° seed beads, 6 g (D)**

**Aqua size 11° seed beads, 10 g (E)**

**Gold size 11° seed beads, 2 g (F)**

**Pink/gold size 11° seed beads, 7 g (G)**

**175 chrysolite crystal bicones, 3 mm (H)**

**2 golden shadow crystal navette pendants, 30 x 14 mm**

**Thread**

**Wax**

**Needles**

**Scissors**

## FINISHED SIZE

**Adjustable to 36½ inches (92.7 cm)**

## TECHNIQUES

**Right angle weave**

**St. Petersburg chain**

# LEAF SLIDE NECKLACE

**A feathery St. Petersburg chain features an elegant cluster of right-angle-weave leaves at one end and crystal navettes on the other. Slide the navettes through any of the leaf shapes for myriad wearing options. A different color on each side makes the necklace even more interesting.**

## Leaf, Side 1

*Row 1:* Use single thread and E beads to make a strip of right angle weave three units long. Step up through the final side E bead.

*Row 2:* Continuing in right angle weave, stitch unit 1 with one E bead for the top, one E bead for the bottom, and one A bead for the side (figure 1). Work units 2 and 3 with all E beads. Exit from the outer side E bead of the final unit.
*Note:* The difference in bead sizes will start the inside curve of the ellipse.

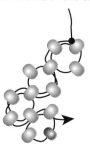

**figure 1**

*Row 3:* Still working in right angle weave, use all E beads for unit 1; make unit 2 with a side E bead and a bottom A bead; and use all A beads for unit 3 (figure 2).

**figure 2**

*Rows 4–14:* Follow the same pattern as row 3, using E beads for the two outside units of the curve and A beads for the inside unit of the curve.

*Rows 15 and 16:* Use all E beads (figure 3).

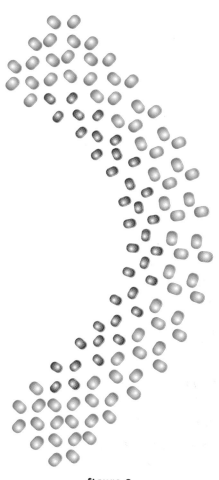

**figure 3**

## Leaf, Side 2

*Row 4: Note:* This is row 4. Rows 1, 2, and 3 are formed by side 1, rows 14–16. Weave through beads to exit from the inside edge E bead of side 1, row 16. Work three units along the inside edge of side 1, working unit 1 with E beads, unit 2 with one E bead and one A bead, and unit 3 with two A beads (figure 4).

**figure 4**

### THE WAY IT MOVES
You can thread the navettes through any of the openings, and the leaves will slide up and down the length of the lariat.

*Rows 5–12:* Repeat rows 5–12 of side 1.

*Row 13:* Join the top beads of row 12 to the bottom beads of side 1 (figure 5). Secure the thread and trim. Set the leaf aside.

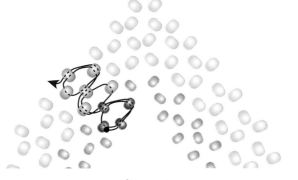

**figure 5**

## Additional Leaves

Complete four additional leaves using E and A beads. Along with the one already made, these will be the five leaf fronts.

To make the leaf backs, complete five leaves using B beads on the inside edge and D beads on the outside edge (figure 6).

**figure 6**

## Join the Front and Back of Leaves

Attach a new thread that exits from an inside edge A bead of one leaf front. Hold this piece and a leaf back together at their inside edges, folding each outside edge away from one another to make the inside beads available for joining. Pick up one A bead and pass through the corresponding B bead of the leaf back. Pick up one A bead; pass through the original B bead, the first A bead just added, and the next B bead on the inside edge of the leaf back (figure 7). Repeat the join until all of the inside edge beads of the leaf front and back are connected.

Join the outside edges in the same way as the inside edges, this time using H beads (figure 8). Set aside.

Repeat to join a total of five leaves.

**figure 7**

**figure 8**

## Leaf Edges

Weave through beads to exit from an outside edge bead on the leaf back. Pick up one A bead and pass through the next edge bead; repeat around the outside edge. If desired, repeat along the inside edge (figure 9). Repeat to add edging beads to the leaf front, this time using B beads. Secure the thread and trim.

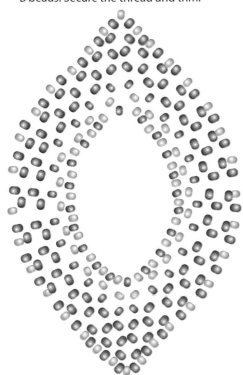

figure 9

Repeat this step for the remaining four leaves. For variety, you could stitch a second row of B embellishment beads opposite the ones on the inside edge.

## Double St. Petersburg Chain

**1** Using double thread, pick up five G beads; pass through the first, second, and third G beads (figure 10) and pull tight to align the beads into two columns.

figure 10

**2** Pick up one E bead and one C bead; pass back through the E bead and the three G beads in the column. Pick up one F bead and pass up through the two G beads in the next column (figure 11).

figure 11

**3** Pick up four G beads; pass through the first two G beads again (figure 12) and pull tight to align into two columns.

figure 12

**4** Pick up one E bead and one C bead; pass back through the E bead and the three G beads in the column. Pick up one F bead and pass through the two G beads in the next column (figure 13).

figure 13

**5** Repeat steps 3 and 4 until the chain measures 32 inches (81.3 cm). You've now finished side 1. Don't trim the thread.

**6** Now you'll start side 2 of the chain. Start a new double thread to pick up five G beads; pass through the first, second, and third G beads and pull tight to align the beads into two columns. Pass through the first F bead from side 1 (figure 14).

figure 14

**7** Pick up four G beads; pass back through the first and second G beads (figure 15). Pull tight to align the beads into two columns.

**figure 15**

**8** Pick up one E bead and one C bead. Pass back through the E bead, the next three G beads in the column below, the shared F bead from side 1, and the two G beads in the next column (figure 16).

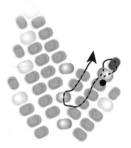

**figure 16**

**9** Repeat steps 7 and 8 for a total of 30 inches (76.2 cm).

**10** Split the chain by continuing to work steps 3 and 4 for an additional 9 inches (22.9 cm), but begin adding an F bead instead of sharing the F bead from side 1. Don't trim the thread. Repeat to

stitch a second single 10-inch (25.4 cm) chain from the double chain (figure 17).

**figure 17**

## Navettes

Exiting from the last two-bead column of one of the single chains, pick up 12 C beads and one navette pendant; pass back through the last G beads exited at the end of the chain. Repeat the thread path to reinforce. Secure the thread and trim.

Repeat this step to add the second navette to the end of the other chain (figure 18).

**figure 18**

## Assemble

Position the leaves in a pleasing pattern. Start a new double thread that exits through an edge bead on one leaf. Pass through an adjacent edge bead on a second leaf. Stitch through two or three adjacent beads to form a strong connection. Weave through beads to exit from the next edge where adjacent leaves touch and repeat the connection. Repeat to join all of the leaves.

Start a new double thread at the end of the double St. Petersburg chain. Pass through two or three edge beads at the top of the leaves, then weave through the opposite side of the chain. Repeat two or three times for a strong connection (figure 19).

**figure 19**

## SUPPLIES

Dark gray size 15° seed beads, 1 g (A)

Silver size 15° seed beads, 1 g (B)

Silver size 11° seed beads, 2 g (C)

Dark silver size 11° seed beads, 4 g (D)

Tan/blue size 11° seed beads, 10 g (E)

11 black diamond crystal lochrose beads, 4 mm (F)

1 silver night crystal flat teardrop pendant, 28 mm

1 silver shade crystal disk pendant, 38 mm

1 pewter bail, 11 x 5 mm

1 silver jump ring, 8 mm

1 silver toggle clasp, 16 mm

Thread

Wax

Needles

Scissors

## FINISHED SIZE

Pendant, 4 inches (10.2 cm) long

Necklace, 30 inches (76 cm) long

## TECHNIQUES

Right angle weave

St. Petersburg chain

Spiral rope

# ELLIPTICAL DISK NECKLACE

Gracefully curved right angle weave is at the centerpiece of this sparkling pendant with a certain Art Deco flair. You'll also get to try your hand at a few more stitches, including double St. Petersburg chain for the bail holding the pendant on the spiral rope.

## Side 1

*Row 1:* Use a single thread and C beads to make a strip of right angle weave three units wide.

*Row 2:* Continuing in right angle weave, make unit 1 with one C bead for the top, one C bead for the bottom, and one A bead for the side (figure 1). Work units 2 and 3 with all C beads. Exit from the outer side C bead of the final unit.
*Note:* The difference in bead sizes will start the inside curve of the ellipse.

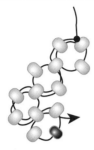

**figure 1**

## Side 2

*Row 4: Note:* This is row 4. Rows 1, 2, and 3 are formed by side 1, row 16. Weave through the beads to exit from the inside edge C bead of side 1, row 16. Work three units along the inside edge of side 1, working unit 1 with C beads, unit 2 with one C bead and one A bead, and unit 3 with two A beads (figure 4).

*Row 3:* Make unit 1 with all C beads; unit 2 with one side C bead and a bottom A bead; and unit 3 with two A beads (figure 2).

**figure 2**

*Rows 4–14:* Follow the same pattern as row 3, using C beads for the outside and A beads for the inside of the curve.

*Rows 15 and 16:* Use all C beads (figure 3).

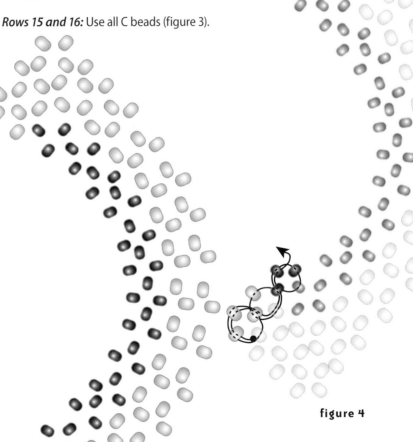

**figure 4**

**figure 3**

### THE WAY IT MOVES
This piece has lots of motion. The pendant slides along the spiral rope; the crystal disk spins, captured inside its seed-bead setting; and a faceted drop dangles below, catching light.

**Rows 5–12:** Repeat rows 5–12 of side 1.

**Row 13:** Join the top beads of row 12 to the bottom beads of side 1 (figure 5). Secure the thread and trim. Set the ellipse aside.

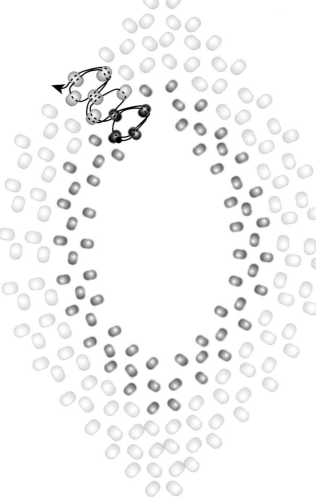

**figure 5**

Make a second, identical ellipse.

## Join the Ellipses

Hold the two ellipses together at their inside edges, folding each outside edge away from the other to make the inside beads available for joining. Pick up one B bead; pass through the corresponding A bead of the second ellipse. Pick up one B bead; pass through the original A bead, the first B bead added, the next A bead, the B bead just added, and the next A bead on the inside edge. Repeat the join, adding one B bead each time until all the inside edge beads are joined (figure 6).

**figure 6**

## Edge

Weave through beads to exit from a C bead on the outside edge of one of the ellipses. Pick up one B bead and pass through the next C bead; repeat around (figure 7). Secure the thread and trim. Set the double ellipse aside.

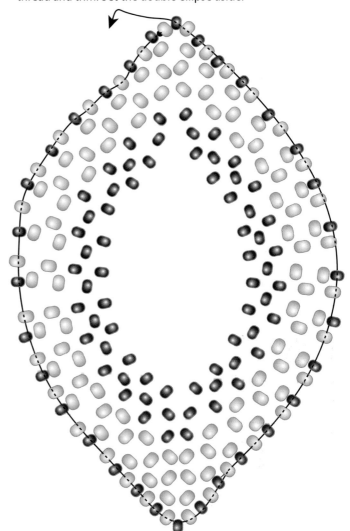

**figure 7**

## Bail Base

**1** You'll work double St. Petersburg chain. Start by using double thread and pick up five C beads; pass through the first three C beads again (figure 8). Pull to align the beads into two columns.

**figure 8**

**2** Pick up one C bead and one A bead; pass back through the C bead and down through the three C beads in the column. Pick up one D bead and pass up through the two C beads in the next column (figure 9).

**figure 9**

**3** Pick up four C beads; pass through the first two C beads again (figure 10). Pull to align the beads into two columns.

**figure 10**

**4** Pick up one C bead and one A bead; pass back through the C bead and down through the three C beads below. Pick up one D bead and pass up through the two C beads in the next column (figure 11).

**figure 11**

**5** Repeat steps 3 and 4 an additional 10 times for a total of 12 stitches.

**6** Use a new double thread to start and pick up five C beads; pass through the first three C beads again (exactly as in figure 8). Pick up one C bead and one A bead; pass back through the C bead and the three C beads below. Pass through the first D bead from side 1 and up through the two C beads in the next column (figure 12).

**figure 12**

**7** Pick up four C beads and pass through the first two C beads again. Pull to align the beads into two columns (figure 13).

**figure 13**

**8** Pick up one C bead and one A bead; pass back through the C bead and down through the three C beads below. Pass up through the next D bead from side 1 and up through the two C beads in the next column (figure 14).

**9** Repeat steps 7 and 8 for the length of side 1. Secure the thread and trim.

## Make the Bail Point and Embellish

**10** Start a new double thread that exits from the first left column. Pick up three C beads; pass through the first two beads on the right column to form a picot at the point of the chain. Continue through two beads on the second column and the one shared D bead in the middle (figure 15).

**11** Pick up one F bead and one A bead; pass back through the F bead and the next shared D bead (figure 16). Repeat for the length of the column, for a total of 11 F beads. Secure the thread and trim.

## Connections

**12** Position the double ellipse inside the disk pendant. Start a new double thread at the bottom of the front ellipse. Pass through two C beads at the point of the front ellipse, pick up four C beads, and pass through the corresponding two C beads on the back ellipse. Pass through the adjacent two C beads on the back of the ellipse. Pick up four C beads and pass through the corresponding two C beads

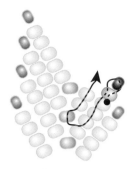

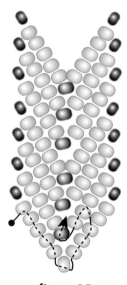

**figure 14**

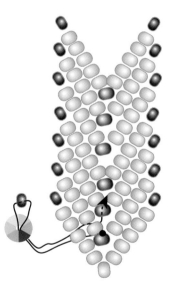

**figure 15**

**figure 16**

on the front of the ellipse. Repeat the thread path to reinforce, securely connecting the bottom of the front and back ellipses. Repeat the same join at the top of the two ellipses (figure 17).

**figure 17**

**13** Fold the double St. Petersburg chain in half to form the bail. Start a new double thread that exits out through the third and second beads at the bottom of the right column. Pass through two C beads at the point of the front ellipse. Pass through two adjacent C beads on the ellipse and the second and third C beads of the left column. Repeat on the back of the bail and the back ellipse (figure 18).

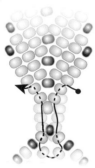

**figure 18**

**14** Connect the metal bail to the teardrop pendant. Use the jump ring to connect the bail to the bottom of the ellipse (figure 19).

**figure 19**

## Spiral Rope

**15** Use single thread and pick up four D beads (these will be called the core) and three E beads (these qualify as a loop). Pass through the four D beads (figure 20).

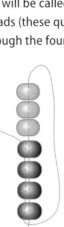

**figure 20**

**16** Pick up one D bead and three E beads; pass up through the top three D core beads and the D bead just added. Use your fingers to push the three E loop beads to the side (figure 21). Repeat this step until you've made the desired length of rope.

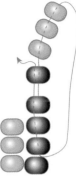

**figure 21**

**17** Pick up seven A beads and pass through the hole in the toggle bar; pass back through the end of the spiral rope. Repeat the thread path several times to reinforce. Secure the thread and trim. Start a new double thread at the other end of the spiral rope and repeat to add the toggle ring.

**18** Slide the spiral rope through the beaded bail.

## SUPPLIES

**Beige-lined size 15° seed beads, 1 g (A)**

**Matte cream size 11° seed beads, 23 g (B)**

**Light sea foam green–lined size 11° seed beads, 7 g (C)**

**105 matte sea foam green size 11° peanut beads (D)**

**Gold-lined size 8° seed beads, 1 g (E)**

**9 chrysolite crystal bicones, 3 mm (F)**

**1 sand opal lochrose bead, 4 mm**

**1 bronze shade crystal rondelle, 12 mm**

**1 green patterned shell donut disk, 34 mm outside diameter, 14 mm inside diameter**

**Thread**

**Wax**

**Needles**

**Scissors**

## FINISHED SIZE

**Top edge, 17 inches (43.2 cm) long**

## TECHNIQUES

**Netting**

**Chevron stitch**

**Right angle weave**

**Peyote stitch**

### THE WAY IT MOVES
A beaded rivet has a loose hold on a shell disk, keeping it attached to the netting yet allowing it to revolve.

# ROUND AND ROUND COLLAR

A spinning shell disk is the focus of this beautiful, softly draping collar stitched with vertical netting.

## Chevron Chain

*Loop 1:* Use double thread to pick up one C bead and pass back through it to form a stop bead. Pick up one C bead, four B beads, and one C bead; pass back through the first C bead to form a loop.

*Loop 2:* Pick up two B beads and two C beads; pass back through the fourth B bead added in the previous loop.

*Loop 3:* Pick up three B beads and one C bead; pass through the first C bead added in the previous loop.

*Loops 4–91:* Repeat loops 2 and 3 for a total of 91 loops (figure 1). *Note:* You can determine how many loops you've completed by counting the sets of two B beads at the top of the chain.

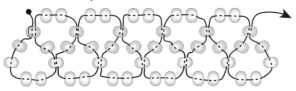

**figure 1**

## Netting

*Net 1:* Weave through beads to exit from the two B beads of the final loop on the bottom of the chevron chain, toward the work. Pick up one C bead, three B beads, one C bead, three B beads, one C bead, and three B beads; pass back through the last C bead added to form a picot. Pick up three B beads, one C bead, and three B beads; pass back through the first C bead added in this net, then pass through the two B beads at the base of the next loop of the chevron chain to form a diamond shape.

*Net 2:* Pick up one C bead and three B beads; pass through the nearest C bead of the previous strand. Pick up three B beads, one C bead, and three B beads; pass back through the last C bead added to form a picot. Pick up three B beads, one C bead, and three B beads; pass back through the first C bead added in

this net, then pass through the two B beads at the base of the next loop of the chevron chain (figure 2).

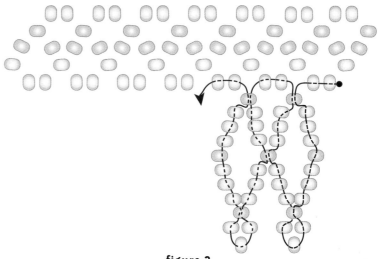

**figure 2**

*Nets 3–13:* Repeat net 2 twelve times, for a total of 13 nets.

*Net 14:* Pick up one C bead and three B beads; pass through the nearest C bead of the previous net. Pick up the following four times: one C bead and three B beads. Pass back through the last C bead added to form a picot. Pick up three B beads, one C bead, and three B beads; pass back through the third C bead added in this net. Pick up three B beads, one C bead, and three B beads; pass back through the first C bead added in this net, then pass through the two B beads at the base of the next loop of the chevron chain (figure 3).

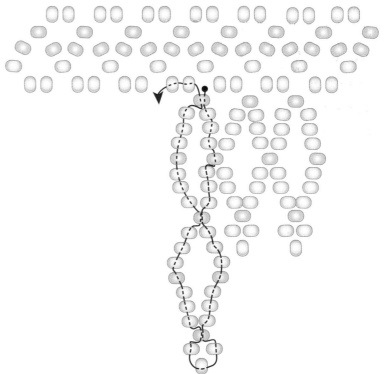

**figure 3**

*Nets 15–40:* Repeat net 14 twenty-six times.

*Net 41:* Pick up one C bead and three B beads; pass through the nearest C bead of the previous net. Pick up the following four times: one C bead and three B beads. Then pick up one C bead, one F bead, and three A beads; pass back through the F and C beads added to form a picot. Pick up three B beads, one C bead, and three B beads; pass back through the fourth C bead added in this net. Pick up three B beads, one C bead, and three B beads; pass back through the second C added in this net. Pick up three B beads, one C bead, and three B beads; pass back through the first C bead added in this net, then pass through the two B beads at the base of the next loop of the chevron chain.

*Nets 42–45:* Repeat net 41 four times, increasing one set of this sequence—three B, one C, and three B beads—for each net. Net 45 will have 7 diamonds.

*Nets 46–91:* Repeat nets 44–14 in reverse, then repeat net 1 to finish the sequence. Figure 4 shows the center of the necklace.

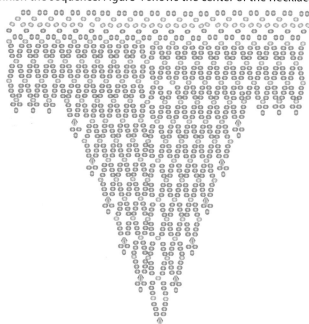

**figure 4**

## Embellish the Chevron Chain

Weave through beads to exit from the first set of two B beads at the base of the chevron chain, toward the work. Pick up one D bead and pass through the next set of two B beads; repeat for the entire length of the chain (figure 5).

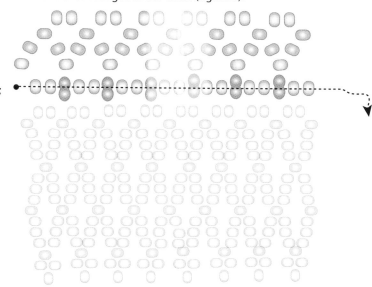

**figure 5**

## Clasp

*Bar:* Start a new double thread that exits from the second set of two B beads at the base of the chevron chain. Pick up the rondelle, the lochrose bead, and one A bead; pass back through the lochrose bead, the rondelle, and the last two B beads exited on the base. Repeat the thread path to reinforce. Secure the thread and trim.

*Ring:* Start a new double thread that exits from the second set of two B beads at the other end of the chevron chain's base. Pick up 28 C beads; pass through the two B beads last exited and the first two C beads just added. Pick up one B bead, skip one C bead in the loop, and pass through the next C bead; repeat around. Secure the thread and trim (figure 6).

**figure 6**

## Spinner Base

*Rows 1 and 2:* Use a single thread and A beads to create a strip of right angle weave 13 units wide and two rows long.

*Row 3:* Use C beads and right angle weave to stitch the row.

*Row 4:* Weave through beads to exit from the bottom A bead of the first unit of row 1. Use C beads and right angle weave to stitch the row (figure 7). Exit through a C bead on the edge of the ring.

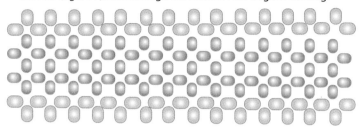

**figure 7**

Join the strip into a tube (figure 8). ***Note:*** Because the bead-work is now tubular, repetitions will be referred to as rounds.

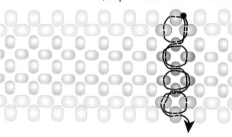

**figure 8**

*Round 5:* Pick up one D bead and pass through the next C bead of the previous round; repeat for a total of 14 D beads. Step up through the first D bead added in this round.

*Round 6:* Pick up one E bead and pass through the next D bead; repeat for a total of 14 E beads. Weave through beads to exit from a C bead at the edge of round 3 (figure 9).

**figure 9**

*Round 7:* Slide the thin side of the beadwork through the center of the shell disk so the flared side touches the patterned side of the shell. Work 14 tubular peyote stitches with one B bead in each stitch; step up through the first B bead added in this round.

*Round 8:* Work 14 tubular peyote stitches with one E bead in each stitch; step up through the first E bead added in this round.

*Round 9:* Work 14 tubular peyote stitches with two B beads in each stitch; step up through the first two B beads added in this round.

*Round 10:* Work 14 tubular peyote stitches with one E bead in each stitch; step up through the first E bead added in this round.

*Round 11:* Work 14 tubular peyote stitches with two C beads in each stitch (figure 10).

**figure 10**

Use the working thread to securely stitch round 11 to the center of the netting, passing through adjacent beads on the netting (figure 11). Secure the thread and trim.

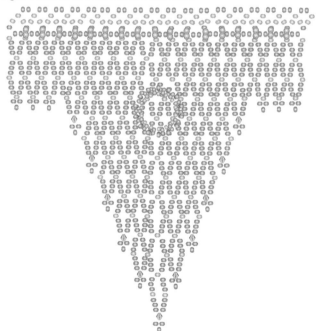

**figure 11**

Gold size 13° charlottes, 1 g (A)

Gold size 15° seed beads, 1 g (B)

Bronze size 15° seed beads, 1 g (C)

Matte blue metallic size 11° seed beads, 1 g (D)

Matte lavender size 11° seed beads, 1 g (E)

Matte green/gold metallic size 11° seed beads, 2 g (F)

Matte green/gold metallic size 8° seed beads, 1 g (G)

Matte blue metallic size 8° seed beads, 1 g (H)

10 violet opal crystal bicones, 4 mm (I)

24 gold aurum crystal bicones, 3 mm (J)

12 Pacific opal crystal bicones, 4 mm (K)

12 turquoise/silver/gold dotted pressed-glass daggers, 7 x 14 mm

1 topaz crystal foil-backed rivoli, 14 mm

1 gray shell donut, 35 mm outside diameter, 15 mm inside diameter

28 inches (71.1 cm) of dark brass mesh chain, 7 mm

2 dark brass end caps with a loop, 8 x 12 mm

1 dark brass toggle clasp with jump rings, 15 mm

Thread

Wax

Needles

Scissors

Chain-nose pliers

Two-part jeweler's epoxy

### FINISHED SIZE

Pendant, 2¼ inches (5.7 cm)

Necklace, adjustable to 26 inches (66 cm)

### TECHNIQUES

Ladder stitch

Peyote stitch

110

# PASSION FLOWER BOLO

Sandwich ladder-stitched spokes together and secure them with a bezeled rivoli to make this sparkling beaded bloom. Adding a beaded band allows it to slide up and down a pretty mesh chain.

## Front Spoke

**1** Use double thread to pick up a stop bead and pass back through it, leaving a 12-inch (30.5 cm) tail. Pick up three G beads and three E beads. Pick up the following sequence eight times: six G beads and three E beads. Then pick up three G beads for a total of ten groups of three E beads. Don't push the beads all the way to the stop bead; leave some slack in the thread. Pass back through the ninth, eighth, seventh, and sixth beads from the end of the initial strand (figure 1). Pull tightly to align the beads in two three-bead columns.

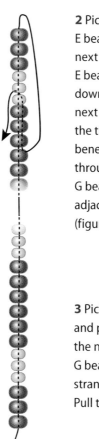

**figure 1**

**2** Pick up five E beads, skip the next middle E bead, then pass down through the next E bead and the three G beads beneath it. Pass up through the three G beads of the adjacent column (figure 2).

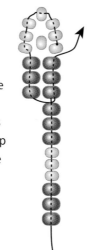

**figure 2**

**3** Pick up one I bead and pass through the next three G beads in the strand (figure 3). Pull tightly to align.

**figure 3**

**4** Pass through the next three G beads in the strand and the next E bead (figure 4).

**figure 4**

**5** Repeat steps 2, 3, and 4 until all of the beads in the strand have been stitched.

**6** Close the beadwork into a ring by passing through the three edge G beads in the final column and the three edge G beads in the first column. Pick up one I bead and pass through the six E beads of the last and first columns again (figure 5).

**figure 5**

**7** Reinforce the spokes of the wheel by passing down through a left-hand column set of G beads toward the center, then picking up three F beads and passing up and then down through the next two columns of G beads. Repeat around (figure 6). Secure the thread and trim; set aside.

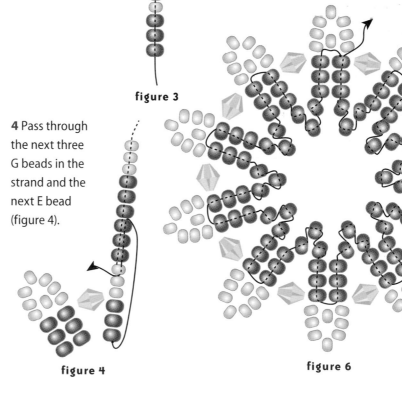

**figure 6**

## THE WAY IT MOVES
This piece of beadwork glides along the mesh rope.

## Back Wheel

**8** You'll complete a second wheel, this time using H, D, and K beads and forming 12 spokes. To form the initial strand, pick up three H beads and three D beads. Pick up the following 11 times: six H beads and three D beads. Pick up three H beads.

**9** Repeat steps 1 to 6. To reinforce the spokes, pass down through a left-hand column set of H beads, pick up five F beads, and pass up, then down through the next columns of H beads. Repeat around (figure 7).

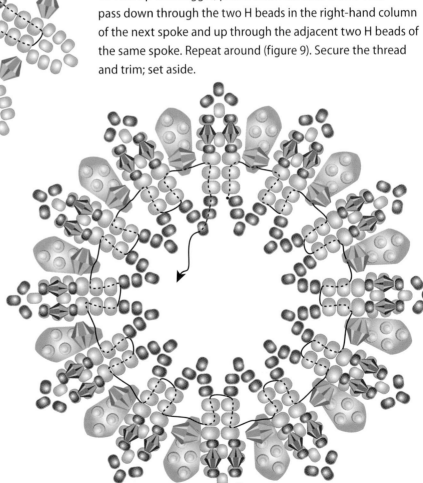

**figure 7**

**10** Exiting from an H bead at the top of the right-hand column of one of the spokes, pick up one C, one J, and one C bead; pass through the middle bead of the nearest group of five D beads. Pick up three F beads and pass through the last D bead exited to form a picot. Pick up one C, one J, and one C bead and pass down through the left-hand column of three H beads in the same column. Pass up through the three right-hand H beads of the next column. Repeat around (figure 8). On the last column, exit from the second H bead of the right-hand column.

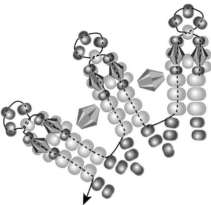

**figure 8**

**11** Pick up one dagger, pass behind the nearest K bead, then pass down through the two H beads in the right-hand column of the next spoke and up through the adjacent two H beads of the same spoke. Repeat around (figure 9). Secure the thread and trim; set aside.

**figure 9**

## Center Rivoli Bezel

**12** Use single thread and B beads to stitch a strip of right angle weave 18 units wide and three rows long. Join the short ends to form a ring, exiting from an edge bead of row 1 (figure 10).

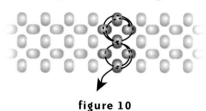

**figure 10**

**13** Pass through all of the beads on the long edge of row 1 and pull tightly to gather, forming a cup. Place the rivoli face up into the cup. Weave through the beads to exit from an edge bead of row 3. Pick up one A bead and pass through the next B bead; repeat around.

**14** Weave through the beads to exit from a bottom bead of row 3. Pick up one E bead and pass through the next bottom B bead of row 3; repeat around (figure 11).

**figure 11**

**15** Weave through the beads to exit from an edge B bead on the back of the bezel. Pick up one B bead and pass through the next B bead on the bezel's edge; repeat once. Continue to work peyote stitch off of the bezel to form a strip of B beads four beads wide and 40 rows long, or an even number that's long enough to wrap a double width of your mesh chain plus two extra rows to allow for stacking the shell donut. *Note:* The peyote strap on the bezel needs to provide enough friction against the mesh chain so that it stays in place when slid into position. Test the fit before attaching to the other side of the bezel.

**16** Interlock the last rows of the strip to the B beads in the other edge of the bezel's back. Weave the beads together to form a seamless join (figure 12). The slider is now finished.

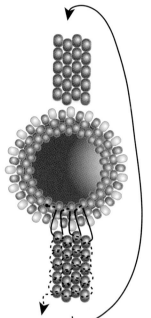

**figure 12**

## Assemble

Use two-part epoxy to glue one end cap to each end of the mesh chain, then use chain-nose pliers to connect one half of the clasp to each end cap; set aside. Stack the front wheel, the back wheel, and the shell donut (figure 13). Place the bezel's band through the center of the stack. Pair the ends of the chain together and pass the ends through the bezel band. Push the slider to the desired level to even up the sides.

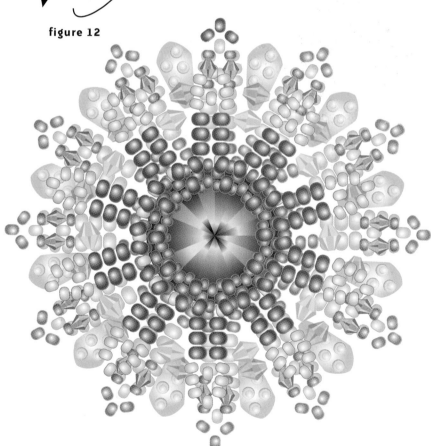

**figure 13**

## SUPPLIES

Silver size 15° seed beads, 2 g (A)

Blue iris size 15° seed beads, 1 g (B)

Blue size 11° seed beads, 4 g (C)

Dark blue size 11° cylinder beads, 6 g (D)

Matte blue size 11° cylinder beads, 6 g (E)

16 blue metallic crystal bicones, 3 mm (F)

33 silver argent AB crystal bicones, 3 mm (G)

15 clear crystal lochrose beads, 3 mm (H)

44 indigo crystal round beads, 2 mm (I)

172 clear crystal round beads, 2 mm (J)

1 silver argent AB crystal teardrop bead, 13 x 8 mm

3 aluminum rings, 26 mm outer diameter, 20 mm inner diameter

Thread

Wax

Needles

Scissors

Flush cutters

Chain-nose pliers, 2 pairs

Cocktail straw

## FINISHED SIZE

Pendant, 3 inches (7.6 cm) long

Necklace, 28 inches (71.1 cm) long

## TECHNIQUES

Right angle weave

Peyote stitch

Russian spiral

# RINGS OF SATURN NECKLACE

With rings orbiting a highly embellished central structure that might be part onion dome, part space satellite as imagined in the 1950s, this spectacular pendant is all mystery—until you follow along with the instructions!

## Ring 1

**1** Make one aluminum ring smaller by using the flush cutters to trim approximately 1⁄16 inch (2 mm) from each side of the split. Use two pairs of chain-nose pliers to form the ring back into a round.

**2** Use single thread and A beads to stitch a strip of right angle weave approximately 27 rows long and six rows wide. *Note:* Tension, thread choice, and bead choice may all affect the length. To test for fit, place the first row of 27 beads around the circumference of the aluminum ring. The strip should be about one bead space short; adjust your count accordingly. If you need to adjust the length, be sure to do it in two-unit increments for an odd count. This note applies to all the rings. When joined, the strip will have an even number of spaces for embellishing. This is important for embellishing every other space differently.

**THE WAY IT MOVES**
Sparkling rings revolve on a beaded core, while the pendant slides along the Russian netted rope. Even the teardrop bead at the bottom swivels!

**3** Join the two short ends into a ring (figure 1).

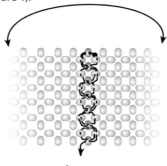

figure 1

**4** Position the strip of beadwork on the interior of the aluminum ring. You don't need to fit the entire ring inside; it will adjust as you complete the join. Use I beads to join the long ends around the aluminum ring (figure 2). Secure the thread and trim. Set the ring aside.

figure 2

## Ring 2

**5** Use single thread and A beads for the top and bottom of each unit and B beads for the sides of each unit to bead a strip of right angle weave approximately 29 units long and six rows wide. *Note:* Don't forget that if you need to adjust the length, you should do it in two-unit increments for an odd count.

**6** Join the two short ends with A beads (figure 3).

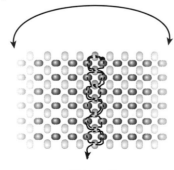

figure 3

**7** Position the strip of beadwork on the interior of an aluminum ring; use B beads to join the long ends around the ring (figure 4).

figure 4

**8** To embellish, weave through beads to exit from a horizontal bead below the joining round. Pick up one A bead and pass through the next bead on the base, then pick up one J bead and pass through the next bead; repeat, alternating A and J beads, until all of the spaces are embellished. Weave through beads to exit from a horizontal A bead of the middle round. Pick up one G bead and one A bead, pass back through the G bead to form a fringe, pass through the next A bead of the base, then pick up one A bead and pass through the next base bead; repeat, alternating between the fringe and the A beads until all spaces are embellished (figure 5).

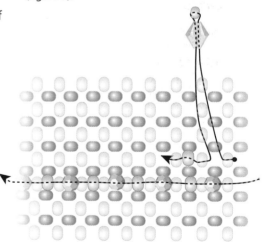

figure 5

**9** Pass through a vertical bead and into a horizontal bead above the middle round. Repeat the first round of embellishment, adding A and J beads every other stitch, taking care that the bead placement in this round matches the bead placement in the first round (figure 6). Secure the thread and trim. Set the ring aside.

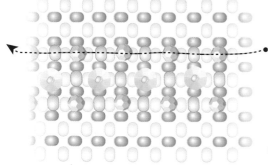

**figure 6**

## Ring 3

**10** Use single thread and A beads to bead a piece of right angle weave that's approximately 31 units long and six rows wide. Join the two short ends with A beads. Position the strip of beadwork on the interior of the ring and join the long edges with A beads (figure 7).

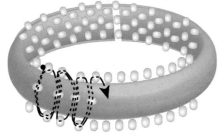

**figure 7**

**11** To embellish, exit from a vertical bead above the joining round. Pick up two A beads, one G bead, and two A beads; pass through the corresponding vertical bead below the joining round, then pass up through the nearest horizontal bead and the next vertical bead. Pick up one J bead, one F bead, and one J bead; pass through the next vertical bead above the

joining round (figure 8). Continue alternating these two groups of beads until the ring is completely covered. Secure the thread and trim. Set the ring aside.

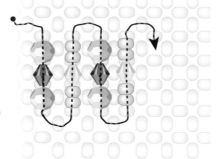

**figure 8**

## Core

You'll make it from the bottom up.

*Rounds 1 and 2:* Use single thread to pick up the following sequence eight times: one D bead and one E bead. Tie a square knot (figure 9).

**figure 9**

*Round 3:* Exiting an E bead, skip one D bead, pick up one D bead, and pass through the following E bead; repeat for a total of 10 D beads. Step up through the first bead added in this round (figure 10).

**figure 10**

*Round 4:* Place eight peyote stitches with one E in each stitch; step up through the first bead added in this round.

*Rounds 5–10:* Work six rounds of peyote stitch, alternating D beads and E beads each round. Always step up through the first bead added in each round.

Work tubular peyote stitch for each round as follows, always stepping up through the first bead or set of beads added in the round unless otherwise indicated:

*Round 11:* Place two D beads in each space (eight beads total).

*Round 12:* Place one E bead in each space.

*Round 13:* Place two D beads in each space.

*Round 14:* Place one E bead in each space.

*Round 15:* Place one D bead, one J bead, and one D bead in each space (figure 11).

**figure 11**

*Round 16:* Place one E bead in each space.

*Round 17:* Place two D beads in each space.

*Round 18:* Place one E bead in each space.

*Round 19:* Place two D beads in each space.

*Rounds 20–24:* Place one bead in each space, alternating E beads and D beads each round.

*Round 25:* Place two D beads in the first space and one D bead in the next space; repeat three times and step up between the first two D beads added in this round.

**Round 26:** Place one E bead between each bead added in the previous round for a total of 12 E beads (figure 12).

figure 12

Place ring 1 on the beadwork. Hold it in place as you work the second ridge. Complete the second ridge as follows, again stepping up through the first bead or set of beads added in the round unless otherwise indicated:

**Round 27:** Place one D bead in each space (12 around).

**Round 28:** Place one E bead in each space.

**Round 29:** Place two D beads in each space.

**Round 30:** Place one E bead in each space.

**Round 31:** Place two D beads in each space.

**Round 32:** Place one E bead in each space.

**Round 33:** Place one D bead, one J bead, and one D bead in each space.

**Round 34:** Place one E bead in each space.

**Round 35:** Place two D beads in each space.

**Round 36:** Place one E bead in each space.

**Round 37:** Place two D beads in each space.

**Round 38:** Place one E bead in each space.

**Round 39–44:** Place one bead in each space, alternating E beads and D beads for each round for a total of six rounds.

Place ring 2 on the beadwork. Hold it in place as you work the third ridge. Create the third ridge as follows, stepping up through the first bead or set of

beads added in the round unless otherwise indicated:

**Round 45:** Place one D bead in each space (12 around).

**Round 46:** Place one E bead in each space.

**Round 47:** Place two D beads in each space.

**Round 48:** Place one E bead in each space.

**Round 49:** Place two D beads in each space.

**Round 50:** Place one E bead in each space.

**Round 51:** Place one D bead, one J bead, and one D bead in each space.

**Round 52:** Place one E bead in each space.

**Round 53:** Place two D beads in each space.

**Round 54:** Place one E bead in each space.

**Round 55:** Place two D beads in each space.

**Round 56:** Place one E bead in each space.

**Round 57–64:** Place one bead in each space, alternating E beads and D beads for each round for a total of eight rounds.

Place ring 3 on the beadwork and hold it in place as you work the fourth ridge. Create the fourth ridge as follows, stepping up through the first bead or set of beads unless otherwise indicated:

**Round 65:** Place two D beads in each space (12 around).

**Round 66:** Place one E bead in each space.

**Round 67:** Place two D beads in each space.

**Round 68:** Place one E bead in each space.

**Round 69:** Place one D bead, one J bead, and one D bead in each space.

**Round 70:** Place one E bead in each space.

**Round 71:** Place two D beads in each space.

**Round 72:** Place one E bead in each space.

**Round 73:** Place two D beads in each space.

**Round 74–76:** Place one bead in each space, alternating E beads and D beads for each round for a total of three rounds.

## Top Loop

Exiting from a D bead of round 76, place one D bead in each of the next two spaces. Turn and continue with flat peyote stitch (figure 13) for 32 rows. Attach the peyote-stitched strip to the mirror beads of round 76 to form a loop.

figure 13

Weave through beads to exit from the second D bead of row 30 of the loop. Pick up one H bead and one A bead; pass back through the H bead and the next D bead of row 29 to form a fringe. Repeat to add five evenly spaced fringes across the loop (figure 14).

figure 14

## Embellish the Core

**Top:** Weave through beads to exit from round 74 of the core. Pick up one A bead and pass through the next bead of round 74; repeat around. Repeat for rounds 73 and 72 (figure 15; for clarity, the top loop isn't shown). Secure the thread and trim.

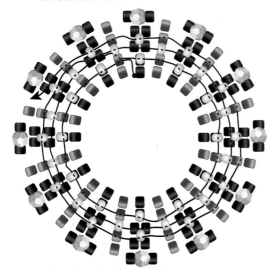

**figure 15**

**Bottom:** Start a new single thread that exits from the core's round 3. Pick up one A bead, one I bead, and one A bead, pass through the next bead in round 3, then pick up one A bead and pass through the next bead of round 3; repeat around. Weave through the beads to exit from a round 5 bead above an I bead just placed. Pick up one D bead and pass through the next round 5 bead, then pick up one I bead and pass through the next round 5 bead; repeat around. Weave through beads to exit from a round 7 bead above an I bead just placed. Repeat the same embellishment as for round 3. Weave through beads to exit from a two-D-bead group of round 11. Pick up one H bead and one A bead, pass back

through the H bead, and pass through the next two D beads of round 11; repeat around (figure 16). Secure the thread and trim.

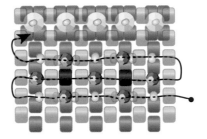

**figure 16**

**Drop:** Thread one needle on each end of a new thread. Pick up one C bead, the crystal teardrop bead from the narrow end, one H bead, and three B beads; pass back through the H bead, the crystal teardrop bead, and the C bead. Both needles should be exiting from the top of the bead group. Pass the needles up through the bottom of the tube on opposing sides, and pass through beads on the core. Pull gently to center the drop (figure 17). Secure the threads and trim. Set the pendant aside.

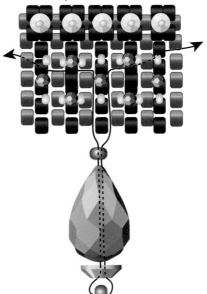

**figure 17**

## Toggle Ring

**Rounds 1 and 2:** Pick up 30 B beads and tie the thread into a ring.

**Round 3:** Pick up one B bead, skip one bead of the previous round, and pass

through the next bead; repeat around for a total of 15 B beads. Step up for the next and subsequent rounds by passing through the first bead added in the current round.

**Round 4:** Place one B bead in each space.

**Rounds 5 and 6:** Place one C bead in each space for a total of two rounds. Weave through beads to exit from round 1.

**Round 7:** Place one C bead in each space.

**Join:** Join the ring on the outer edge by weaving through the beads of rounds 6 and 7.

**Round 8:** Exiting from a round 7 bead, pick up one J bead and pass through the next round 7 bead; repeat for a total of 15 beads.

**Round 9:** Weave through beads to exit from round 6. Pick up one A bead and pass through the next C bead of round 6; repeat for a total of 15 A beads (figure 18). Don't trim the thread; set the toggle ring aside.

**figure 18**

## Toggle Bar

Use single thread and B beads to make a strip of right angle weave nine units long and six rows wide. Join the long ends around a cocktail straw with B beads to form a beaded tube. Cut the straw so it's just slightly shorter than the tube. Exit from a bead on the second round of vertical beads. *Pick up one A bead and pass through the next vertical bead; repeat on the third, ninth, and

10th rounds. Use the A beads just added on rounds 9 and 10 to complete a right-angle-weave unit using J beads as the top and bottom beads. Pass through the nearest end B bead; pass through all six end B beads to close the end. Repeat for rows 2 and 3 (figure 19). Weave through beads to exit from the midpoint of the beaded tube. Don't trim the thread; set aside.

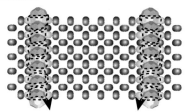

**figure 19**

## Russian Netted Rope

**Round 1:** Use single thread to pick up the following sequence of beads three times: one C bead and two B beads. Exit from the first B bead (figure 20).

**figure 20**

**Round 2, loop 1:** String one C bead and two B beads; skip one B bead and one C bead and pass through the next B bead (figure 21).

**figure 21**

**Round 2, loop 2:** Repeat round 1, loop 1 (figure 22).

**figure 22**

**Round 2, loop 3:** Repeat round 1, loop 1, then step up through the first C and B beads added in this round (figure 23).

**figure 23**

Repeat round 2 until the rope measures 26 inches (66.4 cm), randomly replacing the C bead with a J bead every few rounds. At the end, exit from an edge bead at the end of the rope. Pick up 14 B beads and pass through a B bead on the corresponding side of the rope to form a loop (figure 24). Repeat the thread path to reinforce. Secure the thread and trim. Repeat on the other end.

**figure 24**

## Assemble

Use the working thread attached to the toggle ring to pick up one C bead, one G bead, one C bead, and 10 B beads; pass through the loop at one end of the rope, then back through the C, G, and

C beads (figure 25). Repeat the thread path to reinforce. Secure the thread and trim.

**figure 25**

Use the working thread attached to the toggle bar to pick up one H bead and one B bead; pass back through the H bead, piercing the straw and passing between the beads directly opposite the H bead. Pick up one C bead, one G bead, one C bead, and 10 B beads; pass through the loop at the other end of the rope, then back through the C, G, and C beads (figure 26). Repeat the thread path to reinforce. Secure the thread and trim. Pass the toggle bar end of the rope through the strap on the top of the pendant.

**figure 26**

# GALLERY

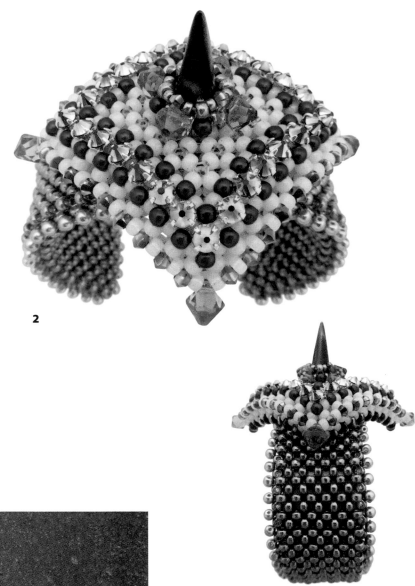

2

### 1. MARTINA NAGELE
*Saturn Goes Bollywood,* 2012
12 x 5 x 5 cm
Seed beads, matte resin beads; right angle weave
Photo by Heiko Radermacher

### 2. SIÂN NOLAN
*The Spike Revolution,* 2012
9 x 7 x 6 cm
Japanese seed beads, Czech pearls, Czech spike bead,
crystal bicones, crystal montées, aluminum cuff
blank; right angle weave, cubic right angle weave
Photos by artist

### 3. ELKE LEONHARDT-RATH
*Eisprinzessin,* 2012
96 cm long; moving wheels, 2.5 cm
Seed beads, crystals, thread; right angle weave,
embellishment
Photo by artist

**4. MET INNMON**
*Flower Pinwheel Encore,* 2011
20 x 15.2 x 1.5 cm
Seed beads, rivolis, bicones, cubes, triangles, thread, wire;
tubular peyote stitch, stringing
Photo by Larry Hansen

**5. MELISSA INGRAM**
*Hepzibah's Pendulum,* 2012
34.5 x 9 x 3.5 cm
Vintage round crystals, crystal pearls, bicones, Czech glass
rondelles, glass drops, seed beads, faceted amethyst pendant, armature ring, thread; cubic right angle weave, right
angle weave, circular peyote stitch, netting, herringbone
stitch, picots
Photo by TWK Studios

**6. TERESA SULLIVAN**
*Cone Lariat,* 2011
57.5 x 5 x 5 cm
Seed beads; sculptural peyote stitch, stringing
Photo by artist

**1. RACHEL NELSON-SMITH**
*Chiclets,* 2011
20.3 x 7.6 x 0.7 cm
Seed beads, crystals, nylon, silver;
right angle weave, tubular peyote stitch
Photo by artist

**2. CYNTHIA NEWCOMER DANIEL**
*Lotus,* 2010
5 x 3.5 cm
Seed beads, crystals; netting, square stitch
Photo by artist

**3. CYNTHIA NEWCOMER DANIEL**
*Wind Dancer 2,* 2012
10 x 2.5 cm
Seed beads, bugle beads, amethyst;
right angle weave, herringbone stitch,
square stitch
Photo by artist

**4. RACHEL NELSON-SMITH**
*Dive,* 2012
30 x 50 x 0.6 cm
Seed beads, thread, sterling silver;
tubular peyote stitch, right angle weave
Photo by artist

5

**5. SABINE LIPPERT**
*Pendulum Necklace,* 2012
Overall, 50 cm; pendants, 7 x 2.5 cm
Seed beads, crystals, pearls, rivolis;
peyote stitch, netting
Photos by artist

**6. NANCY DALE**
*Spring Flowers,* 2011
Pendant, 6.4 cm; rope, 50.8 cm
Seed beads, crystals, pearls, thread, lamp-
worked bead; right angle weave, fringing,
cubic right angle weave, embellishment
Photo by Sherwood Lake Photography

6

123

**1. MIRIAM SHIMON**
*Bollywood,* 2011
20 x 20 x 8 cm
Seed beads, crystals, Czech crystals, rivolis;
netting, peyote stitch
Photo by artist

**2. MIRIAM SHIMON**
*Waterlillies,* 2012
20 x 18 x 6 cm
Seed beads, pearls, Czech glass leaves,
crystals; netting, peyote stitch, fringing
Photo by artist

**3. MIRIAM SHIMON**
*Monet's Garden,* 2011
20 x 18 x 7 cm
Seed beads, crystals, amethyst cabochon;
herringbone stitch, peyote stitch
Photo by artist

**5**

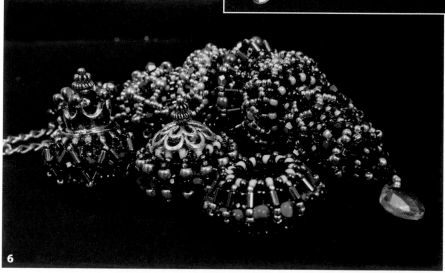

### 4. NANCY CAIN AND MET INNMON
*Beads in Motion,* 2006
49 x 5 x 1 cm
Seed beads, rivolis, thread; tubular peyote
stitch, herringbone stitch
Photo by Dave Wolverton

### 5. PATRICK DUGGAN
*Whirl,* 2012
Necklace, including pendant, 27.5 cm;
pendant, 6.5 cm wide
Rivolis, seed beads, Czech fire-polished beads;
peyote stitch, herringbone stitch, netting
Photo by Neva Brown

### 6. HEATHER COLLIN
*Sabine,* 2012
Pendant, 13.5 x 1 cm
Seed beads, crystals, bugle beads;
cubic right angle weave
Photos by Michael Help

**4**

**6**

## ABOUT THE AUTHOR

Working with her hands to create art has been a lifelong pursuit for Marcia DeCoster. She learned to knit when she was 10, then moved on to crochet, macramé, and embroidery, all of which led the way to beads. After discovering beads and beadweaving in the early 1990s,

Photo by Mark DeCoster

Marcia knew that she had found the one medium that would sustain her creativity. After spending those early years building the fundamental skills of the different stitches, she moved on to developing her own designs and then to sharing those designs through teaching and writing.

Marcia's previous career in information technology left her with an affinity for computer software, which has aided her efforts to become proficient in bead illustration—now a new passion.

Marcia shares her Southern California home with husband Mark and lovable dog Miss Maya. Her three grown children and precious grandchildren provide plenty of opportunity for family visits. Fortunately, Marcia's love of travel is often combined with her love of beads, and she continues to explore the world while meeting fellow beaders.

Marcia's work has been included in *Masters: Beadweaving* and *Showcase 500 Beaded Jewelry*. Her first book, *Marcia DeCoster's Beaded Opulence*, was the second offering in Lark Jewelry & Beading's Beadweaving Master Class series.

## ACKNOWLEDGMENTS

The writing of a book is not a solitary effort. All of those who have contributed to my learning, who have believed in my vision, and who have stood alongside me, taking on tasks to free up my time—all of those people are responsible for this book.

Mark has walked with me, making things possible, for close to 30 years. His quiet strength is invaluable as he lends his advice when needed and provides the extra set of hands required to keep MadDesigns functioning while I write. I couldn't ask for a better or more supportive life partner.

As my journey with beads progresses, I'm thankful for the bead store owners who have believed in me from my earliest designs. Their guidance has always been a source of encouragement and I'm so grateful for their support. Susan, Carole, and Blanche, you are my heroes. Thank you. Thanks go as well to all of those who put their faith in me by inviting me to be part of their beading events.

Along the way, I've developed many meaningful friendships with my bead colleagues and am incredibly thankful for their inspiration and willingness to share information. I'm continually touched by the goodwill of the beading community. I was fortunate a few years ago to meet Jean Campbell, whose elegant grace, technical competence across a range of bead disciplines, and well-placed sense of humor have always been of great assistance. I'm also fortunate to have the friendship of Gabriella van Diepen and Tina Hauer, both of whom sat for long hours and beaded with me, helping to bring my visions to life. Another constant source of support in my beading life is accomplished bead artist Liz Thompson, who has made innumerable samples, has proofread countless directions, and joins me in the classroom every year at the Bead&Button Show in Milwaukee.

As I transitioned to new illustration software, many who were already proficient shared their expertise with me. Rachel Nelson-Smith jump-started my learning with a daylong session of bead drawing. Bonnie Brooks, an accomplished illustrator, was always an email away as I took on each new challenge. Florence Turnour and Cindy Holsclaw also jumped in to help me get unstuck. Each of these people took time out of their schedules to assist me. I find generosity to be the essence of this community.

I'm honored by each of my students who have made the choice to spend their valuable time in the classroom with me. From each of you I gain more insight about the process of teaching, the process of learning, and the art of beading. Teaching is one of the exceptional things I get to do in this life with beads.

I'm also supported by a group of women near my home who share the love of art and the bond of friendship. They are the cheerleaders of my daily efforts to share with you my love for beads. For that I thank you, Gail, Judy, and Susan.

Finally, I would like to thank all of the people at Lark Jewelry & Beading who came together to make this book a reality. Ray Hemachandra, who first listened to my proposal and whose encouragement caused me to move forward, is responsible for nurturing my idea. Nathalie Mornu, who was always a phone call away, offered guidance, finessed my words, and kept me on track.

## CREDITS

**Editor**
Nathalie Mornu

**Art Director & Cover Designer**
Kathleen Holmes

**Illustrator**
Marcia DeCoster

**Photographer**
Stewart O'Shields

**Technical Editor**
Anne Cox

**Editorial Assistants**
Hannah Doyle
Dawn Dillingham

**Art Assistant**
Carol Morse Barnao

**Art Intern**
Tanya Johnson

## INDEX

# AN ESSENTIAL LIBRARY OF BOOKS FOR BEADERS

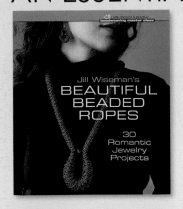

Jill Wiseman's
BEAUTIFUL
BEADED
ROPES
30 Romantic Jewelry Projects

SABINE LIPPERT'S
BEADED
FANTASIES
30 Romantic Jewelry Projects

JAPANESE BEADWORK
WITH SONOKO NOZUE
25 Jewelry Designs from a Master Artist

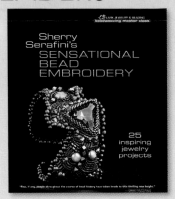

Sherry Serafini's
SENSATIONAL BEAD EMBROIDERY
25 inspiring jewelry projects

MAGGIE MEISTER'S
CLASSICAL ELEGANCE
20 beaded jewelry designs

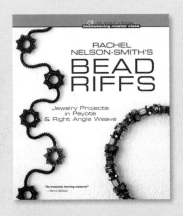

RACHEL NELSON-SMITH'S
BEAD RIFFS
Jewelry Projects in Peyote & Right Angle Weave

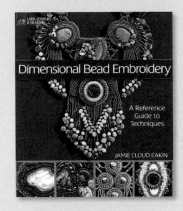

Dimensional Bead Embroidery
A Reference Guide to Techniques
JAMIE CLOUD EAKIN

Diane Fitzgerald's
SHAPED BEADWORK
dimensional jewelry with peyote stitch

Marcia DeCoster's
BEADED OPULENCE
elegant jewelry projects with right angle weave

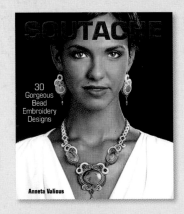

SOUTACHE
30 Gorgeous Bead Embroidery Designs
Anneta Valious

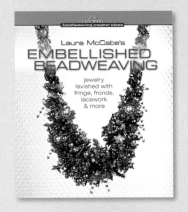

Laura McCabe's
EMBELLISHED BEADWEAVING
jewelry lavished with fringe, fronds, lacework & more

Tapestry Bead Crochet
Projects & Techniques
BONUS DVD INCLUDED
Ann Benson

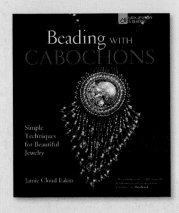

Beading WITH CABOCHONS
Simple Techniques for Beautiful Jewelry
Jamie Cloud Eakin

Metalworking 101 for Beaders
CREATE CUSTOM FINDINGS, PENDANTS & PROJECTS
A Lark Jewelry Book
Candie Cooper

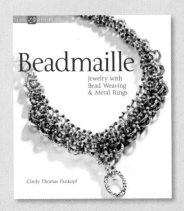

Beadmaille
Jewelry with Bead Weaving & Metal Rings
Cindy Thomas Pankopf

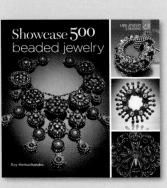

Showcase 500 beaded jewelry
Ray Hemachandra